English Academic Writing for Graduate Students

研究生英语学术论文写作

主 编／金 晶 郑玉琪

编 者／蔡旭东 李 黎 吴 婷
孙书兰 陈峥嵘 凌建辉

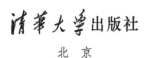

清华大学出版社
北 京

内 容 简 介

本教材以任务型教学为编写原则与核心理念,将论文写作步骤与语言技能训练融为一体,使学术论文写作的知识与实训紧密结合,兼顾各学科论文写作的特色与要求,并提供大量实例,有针对性地设计大量课堂练习,增加教学实效。本教材内容涵盖学术英语写作的各个组成部分,每个单元均设计了与该单元主题相关的思考题、论文实例、语言点、写作技能与写作实践等环节。学生在进行各单元的写作实践后即可完成一篇完整的学术研究论文。本教材另配有相关练习的答案详解及电子课件,读者可登录 www.tsinghuaelt.com 下载使用。

本教材适用于研究生及高年级本科生,也可用作提高英语学术论文写作水平的辅导教材。

图书在版编目(CIP)数据

研究生英语学术论文写作 / 金晶,郑玉琪主编 . — 北京:清华大学出版社,2020.3(2025.3重印)
ISBN 978-7-302-54329-9

Ⅰ.①研… Ⅱ.①金… ②郑… Ⅲ.①英语－论文－写作－研究生－教材 Ⅳ.① H319.36

中国版本图书馆 CIP 数据核字(2019)第 263213 号

责任编辑:刘 艳
封面设计:张伯阳
责任校对:王凤芝
责任印制:丛怀宇

出版发行:清华大学出版社
   网 址:https://www.tup.com.cn, https://www.wqxuetang.com
   地 址:北京清华大学学研大厦 A 座   邮 编:100084
   社 总 机:010-83470000   邮 购:010-62786544
   投稿与读者服务:010-62776969, c-service@tup.tsinghua.edu.cn
   质量反馈:010-62772015, zhiliang@tup.tsinghua.edu.cn
印 装 者:三河市君旺印务有限公司
经 销:全国新华书店
开 本:185mm×260mm   印 张:10.5   字 数:218千字
版 次:2020 年 3 月第 1 版   印 次:2025 年 3 月第 5 次印刷
定 价:56.00 元

产品编号:086020-02

前　言

近年来，国际学术交流日益频繁，高层次国际化人才的培养已成为我国高等教育事业发展的重点。社会需求和学习者的学术发展对高校研究生公共英语教学提出了更严峻的挑战。研究生英语教学的培养目标首先应考虑国际化和国际交流背景下研究生应具备的学术英语应用能力，使其能有效从事本专业学术研究和交流，尤其是要提高其学术英语写作能力，以帮助其在国际学术期刊上发表论文或在国际学术会议及论坛上报告科学研究成果。

学术英语写作能力是学术能力的基本组成部分，包括选题能力、文献检索和阅读能力、语篇构建能力、获取有效信息的能力、语言表达能力等诸多方面。本教材以提高研究生学术英语写作能力为目标，以任务型教学为编写原则和核心理念，将论文写作步骤与语言技能训练融为一体，使知识讲解与写作实训紧密结合，以学习成果为导向，将教学过程设计为任务型项目，兼顾文理科论文写作的特色与要求，提供了丰富的实例兼作阅读样本和写作模板，有针对性地设计了大量课堂练习，提高课堂教学内容与活动的可操作性，增强教学实效，让学生在过程中学会写作。学生在完成每一单元的学习后，不仅能掌握必要的写作知识，而且可以通过模仿练习和实战写作，学会如何写好论文的相关部分。完成全书的学习之后，学生可了解英语学术论文写作的全过程以及学术写作各个环节的写作技能，为完成自己的英语学术论文打下坚实的基础并做好充分的准备。

本教材共分 8 个单元，内容涵盖英语学术论文写作的各个组成部分：学术英语语言特点、开题报告、文献综述、研究方法、数据分析与讨论、研究结论、摘要与参考文献以及致谢与投稿。每个单元均设计了与该单元主题相关的思考题、论文实例、语言点、写作技能和写作实践等环节。教师可用 4 个课时完成一个单元的教学和部分写作练习，学完本教材约需 32 个课内课时，与论文相关的写作实践及文献查阅和分析需要大量的课外时间才能完成。本教材配有丰富的学习资源，学生可扫描封面背后的二维码，注册成功后再扫描正文相应的二维码获得。

本教材的策划、构思与编写得到了东南大学研究生院和外国语学院的大力支持和关心，参编者均为研究生教学部承担一线教学任务的教师。东南大学自 2012 年开始进行研究生公共英语教学改革，学术英语写作课程是其中的一项重要内容。本教材基于该校多年来的教学实践与教改经验编写而成，其相关教学模式与课程改革曾获得江苏省教育厅"研究生教育改革成果二等奖"。

由于编者水平有限，教材中的疏漏之处在所难免，恳请同行和使用者不吝赐教。

编者

2024 年 3 月

于东南大学

Contents

UNIT 5 Results & Discussion ···**73**

UNIT 6 Research Conclusion ·······································**95**

UNIT 1
Academic Writing Style

 Learning Objectives

- To understand the style and features of academic discourse;

- To distinguish between the academic style and the personal style of writing;

- To recognize various levels of formality;

- To use appropriate words and sentences in academic writing.

Warm-up

As a graduate student, you will face a lot of writing tasks as you work toward the chosen degree. Naturally, these tasks vary from one discipline to another. They are, however, similar in one respect—they all need to be completed "academically". What is the academic style? This is a question that students frequently ask. The English language used in writing academic papers differs from that in common writing in many aspects.

To know more about academic writing, think about the following questions first:

- How is academic writing different from other forms of writing?
- What is your purpose of initiating an academic research?
- What are the key characteristics of academic writing?

Sample Reading

What Are the Key Characteristics of Academic Writing?

Compare and contrast the following two pieces of writing.

The first example is an e-mail written by a student, and the second is an essay extract on the same topic.

- Dear Professor,

  Please find below my answers to your questions.

  I think academic English and everyday English are different because they have very different goals. Lectures and seminars need a different approach from spoken English. And, of course, academic essay writing isn't the same as standard writing.

  I think there are four main areas where I can see big differences between standard writing and academic writing. They are as follows:

  - You should not be subjective;
  - You should be more complex;
  - You should have more structures;

- You should use the academic style and system.

Best wishes,

Sophia

- "Academic English" is differentiated from "general English" in its focus on "those communication skills in English which are required for study purposes in formal education systems" (Jordan, 1997: 1). Within these systems, there are three main areas of focus: the lecture, the seminar and the essay, each of which has a specific set of subskills which are required for successful performance. It is essays where the most significant distinction between academic English and general English is made. Generally speaking, there are four main areas where differences between standard writing and academic writing can be observed: the inherent objectivity of academic writing, its complexity, its formality of structure and its adoption of academic style.

It is almost impossible to define good academic writing exactly. However, it is certainly possible to identify some key characteristics. The ones listed below are four of the most important features.

Academic writing:

- is more objective;
- is more complex;
- has a more formal structure;
- uses more referencing.

Academic Writing Is More Objective.

Phrases such as "I think" "I believe" and "in my opinion" should not be used in academic writing. Academics are not looking for what you think or believe—they want to see what you can show, demonstrate and prove through evidence. For example:

- **General writing:** *I think* there are four main areas where *I can see* big differences between standard writing and academic writing.

- **Academic writing:** Generally speaking, there are four main areas where differences between standard writing and academic writing can be observed.

Three specific strategies for achieving objectivity are outlined below:

- **Strategy 1:** Hedging language increases the "distance" between the writer and the text, thereby creating more objectivity.

- **Strategy 2:** Empty introductory phrases provide a platform for objective statements.

- **Strategy 3:** The passive voice removes the need for a subject in the sentence.

Academic Writing Is More Complex.

As a general principle, academic writing is more complex than other forms of writing. This is because academic writing often discusses difficult, challenging ideas which can only be expressed with particular grammar and language. This complexity may be seen in the following three aspects.

Formality of Language

Academic language is more formal than the language used in other forms of writing. For example:

- **General writing:** big differences

- **Academic writing:** the most significant distinction

Grammatical Structures

Some grammatical forms appear more frequently in academic writing than in other forms of writing, like the passive voice, noun phrases and relative clauses. For example:

- **Academic writing:** a specific set of subskills which are required for successful performance

Density of Language

In the two writing samples on Pages 2–3, the average number of letters per word of the e-mail is 4.8, whereas it is 5.4 for the sample of academic writing. This density can be achieved through a greater use of content words (such as verbs and nouns) rather than structure words (such as prepositions and conjunctions). In the example below, the adjective form found in general writing is substituted with a verb form in academic writing.

- **General writing:** Academic English and everyday English *are different*...

- **Academic writing:** "Academic English" *is differentiated from* "general English"...

Academic Writing Has a More Formal Structure.

All forms of writing have a certain type of structure. The structure of academic writing is more formal than that of other forms of writing. The following characteristics can be observed:

- The text as a whole has a specific, formalized structure—the introduction, main body and conclusion.

- The text must have cohesion and coherence—it must link together clearly so that it is possible to follow the writer's argument.

- Paragraphs should be roughly of the same length throughout, so there is a good overall balance.

- Paragraphs often follow a similar structure—topic sentence, outline of argument, supporting evidence, short conclusion and transition to the next paragraph.

Academic Writing Uses More Referencing.

Building on the ideas of other people is one of the central features of academic writing. In order to show where these ideas come from (and to avoid plagiarism), a reference system is used. For example:

- **General writing:** I think academic English and everyday English are different because they have very different goals.

- **Academic writing:** "Academic English" is differentiated from "general English" in its focus on "those communication skills in English which are required for study purposes in formal education systems" (Jordan, 1971:1).

(Adapted from C. Sowton. 2012. *50 Steps to Improving Your Academic Writing*. Reading: Garnet Publishing.)

> **Tasks**

❶ Summarize the key characteristics of academic writing and discuss with a partner about why these features prevail in academic writing.

Key Academic Writing Features	Reasons Behind
Objectivity	
Complexity	
Formal structure	
Referencing	

❷ Match the following writing strategies with the possible features in the box.

a. objectivity   b. complexity   c. formal structure   d. referencing

_____ 1) a reference system

_____ 2) empty introductory phrases

_____ 3) a greater use of content words

_____ 4) the passive voice

_____ 5) cohesion and coherence

_____ 6) relative clauses

_____ 7) hedging language

_____ 8) same-length paragraphs

_____ 9) noun phrases

❸ **Which of the italicized words in each sentence would be more suitable for an academic paper? Write down the correct answers.**

1) The government has made *good/considerable* progress in solving environmental problems.

   _____

2) We *got/obtained* encouraging results.

   _____

3) The results of *a lot of/numerous* different projects have been *pretty good/encouraging*.

   _____

4) A loss of jobs is one of the *things that will happen/consequences* if the process is automated.

   _____

5) The future of Federal funding is *up in the air/uncertain*.

   _____

III Language Focus

A. Word Choice

The English language often has two or more choices to express an action or occurrence. The choice is often between a phrasal verb and a single verb. Often in lectures and other instances of everyday spoken English, the phrasal verb is used; however, for written academic English, the preferred choice is a single verb wherever possible. This is one of the most dramatic shifts from informal style to formal style. Academic voice can be well expressed by choosing words. A distinctive feature of academic writing is choosing the more formal ones when selecting a verb, a noun, or other parts of speech. For example:

- **Less formal style:** Researchers *looked at* the way strain *builds up* around a fault.

- **Academic style:** Researchers *observed* the way strain *accumulates* around a fault.

> **Tasks**

❶ Match the informal expressions in the first column with the formal verbs in the second column. Then write the noun forms of these formal verbs in the third column. The first one is given as an example.

Column 1	Column 2	Column 3
1) find out	verify (10)	verification
2) look at carefully	examine ( )	_____
3) go up and down	establish ( )	_____
4) set up	increase ( )	_____
5) get rid of	investigate ( )	_____
6) cut down	assist ( )	_____
7) help out	discover ( )	_____
8) go up	eliminate ( )	_____
9) look into	reduce ( )	_____
10) make sure something is true	fluctuate ( )	_____

❷ Rewrite the following sentences to make them more formal by substituting the italicized phrase with a single verb.

1) The implementation of computer-integrated-manufacturing (CIM) has *brought about* some serious problems.

_____

2) The process should be *done over* until the desired results are achieved.

_____

_____

3) Plans are being made to *come up with* a database containing detailed environmental information for the region.

_____

_____

4) Subtle changes in the earth's crust were *picked up* by these new devices.

_____

_____

5) Proposals to construct new nuclear reactors have *met with* great resistance from environmentalists.

_____

_____

B. Formal Grammar and Style

Sentence structures in academic writing are more complex than in other forms of writing in that academic writing often discusses difficult, challenging ideas which can only be expressed with particular grammar and language. But do not mistake "complex" for "complicated". Academic writing should not be complicated. It should be relatively easy to follow, and be written in a clear, direct way.

The following are some recommendations for maintaining a formal academic writing style.

First, avoid contractions. For example:

- Export figures *won't* improve until the economy is stronger. (×)
- Export figures *will not* improve until the economy is stronger. (√)

Second, use the more appropriate formal negative forms. For example:

- The analysis *didn't* yield *any* new results. (×)
- The analysis yielded *no* new results. (√)
- The government *didn't* allocate *much* funding for the program. (×)
- The government allocated *little* funding for the program. (√)
- This problem *doesn't* have *many* viable solutions. (×)
- This problem has *few* viable solutions. (√)

Third, limit the use of "run on" expressions, such as "and so forth" and "etc.". For example:

- These semiconductors can be used in robots, CD players, *etc.* (×)
- These semiconductors can be used in robots, CD players, *and other electronic devices.* (√)

Fourth, avoid addressing the reader as "you". For example:

- *You* can see the results in Table 1. (×)

- The results can be seen in Table 1. (√)

Last but not least, limit the use of direct questions. For example:

- What can be done to lower costs? (×)

- We now need to consider what can be done to lower costs./We now need to consider how costs may be lowered. (√)

 Task

Rewrite the following sentences to make them more formal.

1) If you fail the exam, you can't enter the university.

_____

2) So, why did the bridge collapse? There're a lot of reasons.

_____

_____

3) You can clearly see the difference between these two processes.

_____

_____

4) These special tax laws have been enacted in six states: Iowa, Illinois, Ohio, etc.

_____

_____

5) So far there hasn't been much research on how conflict influences the level of trust and respect in a group.

_____

_____

C. Linking Words and Flow

Sentences that are too short and poorly connected can be irritating to read. Linking words and phrases can help a writer maintain flow and establish clear relationships between ideas.

 Task

Rewrite the following paragraph into one with an easy flow.

A conjunction connects words, phrases, or clauses. It indicates the relationship between the elements. These elements connect. We often find the following thing. In only one single sentence a conjunction connects one or more ideas. These ideas may be equal or unequal in importance. Ideas are equal, and we call them coordinate ideas. For example, John studies electronics. Helen studies computing. These two sentences can become a compound sentence. It shows the relationship between the two ideas. We want to maintain the equality of the ideas. We call the clauses in the new sentence coordinate clauses.

_____

_____

_____

_____

_____

_____

_____

_____

_____

A. Recognizing Different Styles

Different styles of writing have different features. Styles may be formal or informal, and will usually vary to fit the audience and the medium of publication. Moreover, the style will also affect how you read and interpret the document concerned. Understanding the writing style will help you put your writing into perspective.

> **Task**

Read the following texts and choose the items from the box to decide where they are taken from.

science magazine	passage from Hemingway's short story *Cat in the Rain*
advertisement	research paper	newspaper

1) At AT & Bell Laboratories infrared lasers are being used to capture live microbes. Working like optical tweezers, the pressure of the laser light traps minute objects in its focus point. Researchers are using the device to move around viruses, bacteria and other cells that they are studying under the microscope. After several hours, however, the focus light will heat up the microbes to a boiling point.

2) All we ask is that you spend two hours of your time attending a Barratt Sales presentation. There, you'll discover the benefits of timeshare. At Barratt we call it Holiday Ownership because that's why it really is. You'll be under no obligation to purchase, but we think you may be tempted.

3) There were only two Americans stopping at the hotel. They did not know any of the people they passed on the stairs on their way to and from their room. Their room was on the second floor facing the sea. It also faced the public garden and the war monument. There were big palms and green benches in the public garden. In the good weather there was always an artist with his easel. Artists liked the way the palms

grew and the bright colors of the hotels facing the garden and the sea.

4) Although many studies have already been done, more studies are needed to determine the effects of microcomputer-assisted instruction in various teaching situations.

5) The parents of a seven-year-old Australian boy woke to find a giant python crushing and trying to swallow him. The incident occurred in Cairns, Queensland and the boy's mother, Mrs. Dryden said, "It was like a horror movie. It was a hot night. He suddenly started screaming. We rushed to the bedroom to find a huge snake trying to strangle him." Mrs. Dryden and her husband, Peter, tried to stab the creature with knives, but the python bit the boy several times before escaping.

B. Choosing Appropriate Styles

Academic texts are usually precise, reliable, formal, and structured because the writers always want to ensure that their work is clearly understood, and there is no room for ambiguity. They also want to justify their point of view. So they support their writing with evidence, either from their own work, or that of others.

> Tasks

❶ **Suppose you are going to write an essay as an assignment. Think about which of the following sentences you would like to use in your writing and why. Then fill in the blanks of the table on the next page.**

1) He couldn't finish his work in the time given.

2) The first set of results were compiled and presented by the other group of students.

3) I would like to focus on the following areas of research: ...

4) They argued that this methodology was unreliable.

5) In addition, the data was used to focus on the following hypothesis.

6) I enjoyed my English class with you and I am having a good experience this semester.

7) At about 12: 00 p.m. on August 21, 1984, she told us, I came out of the kitchen to

toss out some water.

8) We, at any rate, will continue to keep an open mind.

9) Is the menu at that French restaurant giving you trouble? Then you might need the Voice, a hand-held computer that translates spoken English into French, Spanish, German or Italian.

10) There is an emerging consensus that a concerted effort on a national level will be required to capture the glittering prizes that a new technology offers.

No.	Y/N	Reason(s) for Your Decision
1)		
2)		
3)		
4)		
5)		
6)		
7)		
8)		
9)		
10)		

❷ Read the following paragraph about the picture. Then rewrite it in academic style.

Why are there so many jams on the roads these days? One thing is that public transportation like trains is so dear. A long time ago, cars cost a lot, but now, unfortunately, they've got a lot cheaper. Another thing is that driving is a lot nicer than waiting for a bus. The trouble is that if everyone buys a car, the roads get packed.

_____

_____

_____

_____

_____

_____

_____

_____

_____

❸ Read an article or a book extract in your subject area and identify examples to match the characteristics of academic writing in the table. Make a list of these findings for future reference.

Characteristics of Academic Writing	Examples
Use passive voice	
Write with structural complexity	
Avoid a casual style	
Use formal words and phrases	
...	

本章配套资源

UNIT **2**
Research Proposal

Learning Objectives

- To understand the importance and major components of a research proposal;

- To become aware of the use of personal pronouns and nominalization in academic writing;

- To initiate your own research;

- To learn to write a research proposal.

Warm-up

Before you learn the detailed steps to write a research proposal, think about the following questions:

- What is your purpose of initiating an academic research?

- Why do you need to write a research proposal?

- How do you choose a topic?

- Do you often encounter the first and second personal pronouns in academic writing? Why?

Sample Reading

Writing a Research Proposal*

A research proposal is an obvious and essential part of a postgraduate degree application in most parts of the world. It is an outline of your proposed project, whose aim is to present and justify your research idea and explain the practical ways in which you think that this research should be implemented. You need to think very carefully about the scope of your research and be ready to explain how you will complete it within the time frame and the available resources. In addition, research proposals are used to evaluate your expertise in the area in which you wish to conduct research, your knowledge of the existing literature, and how your project will enhance it.

Short-term projects such as those undertaken at the undergraduate or postgraduate diploma level are essential training for graduate research. The transition into a graduate degree, such as a Master's degree or a Ph.D., involves a much higher level of independent thinking and activity than most students realize. A large number of students usually find this transition very challenging and daunting. The challenge starts from the time when applicants are required to write and present a research proposal.

Proposal writing is in fact a process of developing a specific research plan from a

---

* See Appendix 1 on Pages 143–154 for a sample research proposal.

generalized idea to a specifically defined written document and oral presentation. Figure 2-1 illustrates a spiral. The top of the spiral represents the general subject matter that interests you. The bottom of the spiral represents the specific research problem you will solve in your dissertation.

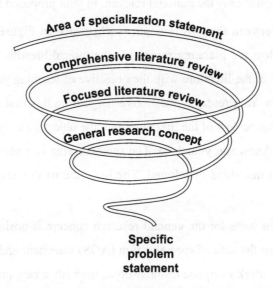

Figure 2-1   The research spiral illustrates the path from a general research interest to a specific research problem.

The area of specialization (AOS) defines the top layer of the three-dimensional spiral, the broad area, and describes the subfields within it or even other disciplines that connect to it. It represents the material you draw from and will eventually contribute to your research. The pieces of the AOS include the subjects or subfields that encompass your work, definitions for those subjects, and a description of the problems addressed or current solutions. Many investigators include more than one subject or subfield. In an era of transdisciplinary research, these subjects can reach into multiple disciplines as well. Here are some examples of subdisciplines from the social sciences: human ecology, demography, linguistic anthropology, and econometrics.

The literature review starts where the AOS left off and digs deeper into those themes by discussing what is known about your particular area, identifying the methods used to investigate those themes, and highlighting what remains unknown.

A literature review is a synthesis (not a summary) of previous work in a specific area or specific areas. A synthesis means you are bringing together different aspects of the literature and creating something new with it. The result is a critical evaluation of the current theory and methods of a particular topic reflecting what is known, how it is known, and what is unknown. The objective of the literature review in a proposal is to provide the reader with the knowledge needed to understand your proposal. It is not an explanation of everything you know about a particular subject. Because of this distinction, you need to perform a thorough investigation of the literature but synthesize only the material relevant to your proposed research.

The difference between the two reviews as illustrated in Figure 2-1 (comprehensive literature review and focused literature review) is the topical breadth. The first version is a comprehensive review of the literature with the objective of teaching yourself what is known about your interest area. Your research questions emerge from this first stage. The second and final version is a focused review of the literature with the objective to inform the reader about what is known and unknown in your area. The research area is a narrower set of literature based on the research questions developed. The outcome of this stage is included in the research proposal.

The document you write for the general research concept is positioned intellectually at the intersection between the area of specialization (AOS) statement and the literature review. It states that within the work everyone else has done, here sits a new problem area that needs to be solved. It aims to answer three basic questions: what, how, and why.

The process begins with *what* and could include one or more of the following questions:

- What else can we know about something?

- What can we do better?

- What is a more complete explanation of something?

And deals with *how*:

- How has this problem been addressed by others?

- How will I do this differently?

And leads to *why*:

- Why do we want to know more about this?

- Why do we need to do it better?

- Why don't we understand this part?

The answers to these basic questions form the basis for the generalized research concept.

The problem statement drills farther down the spiral from a research topic toward a solution you work toward in your dissertation. The research problem (or research statement) refers to a specific instance of a generalized research goal within your area of specialization. The idea that you are solving a problem suggests the problem can be solved. In many cases, research results do not necessarily solve the problem but rather contribute to understanding it better.

There are two distinguishable ways to describe the topic you are going to address: as an objective and as a question. A research objective is a declarative statement describing an outcome-based goal investigating facts, theories, or methods. The outcome is a better understanding into a gap identified in the literature review. A research question is an interrogative statement. Forming a research question is often identified as the initial step in the scientific method. The scientific method refers to a specific approach for investigating a problem or acquiring new knowledge.

The following components are essential in a research proposal, and you are advised to ensure that all are present in your version. However, this is not to say you cannot add a few other details that you feel may be necessary.

A Clear Working Title

Choosing your research topic is probably the first step and most important single decision you have to make in carrying out your research. One of the key skills involved in choosing a topic is to pick one of the appropriate size—neither too big nor too small—and achievable within the time, space, and available resources. The title of the research project given at the proposal level is often referred to as a working title. The reason for this is that it is most likely to change as the work progresses. It is normal for students to refine the original proposal in light of detailed literature reviews, further consideration of research approaches, and comments received from the supervisors and/or other faculty members in the course of the study. Nevertheless, you need to include important keywords that will relate your proposal to relevant supervisors. Try to ensure that your title does not only simply describe the subject matter but also gives an indication of your intended approach; for example, "Optimization of Distributed Generation in Electric Power Systems Using Fuzzy-Genetic Algorithm Approach".

Overview of the Research

A brief overview of your research and the context into which it fits within the existing academic literature should be provided in this section. Be as specific as possible in identifying relevant influences or debates.

Be sure to establish a solid and convincing framework for your research in this section. This should include a clearly articulated research problem, which typically takes the form of concise questions regarding the relationship between two or more variables. In this section, one to three research questions should suffice, and the reason for asking them, as well as the significance of the research. The research problem should be capable of being tested empirically.

Review of Literature

The primary purpose of a literature review is to help you become familiar with the work that has already been carried out in the selected topic area. It is absolutely indispensable when you plan a research study because it would guide you in the appropriate direction by answering several questions related to the topic area: Has anybody worked on this topic area before? If so, what suggestions can you make from the results of the earlier studies? Did they encounter any methodological difficulties which you need to be aware of when planning your own research? Is more research required to be carried out on this topic? If so, in what specific area?

The literature review section should discuss the texts that you believe are most important to the project, demonstrate your understanding of the research issues, and identify existing gaps that your research intends to fill. You should also identify some leading scholars in the field, particularly those whose published works you have studied.

A critical literature review is crucial to ensure that your project does not duplicate work already done without having any knowledge that the same study has already been carried out. You can often save yourself a good deal of time, money, and above all, the embarrassment that might later ensue, by quickly changing the direction of your study if you discover, from your literature review, that the research questions you are planning to conduct have already been answered.

Also, the review of recent related literature could help you discover the latest facilities that are more efficient than earlier existing ones in carrying out your work. Though literature review could initially tend to be intimidating, most other things relating to research become easier when it is done thoroughly, especially as you gain experience.

Research Methodology

The methodology section is a hugely important part of your research proposal. It chronicles the approach(es) you will use to achieve your research results. Incidentally, it is the portion of the proposal that most students find the most difficult. For that reason, you may wish to take a look at some past related theses to ensure that you know the appropriate way to do things. In any case, this section should lay out, in clear terms, the way in which you will structure your research and the specific methods you will use. A well-developed methodology section is crucial. Make sure to include specific techniques and not just a general approach. This should include the types of resources consulted, methods for collecting and analyzing data, and you must be able to justify why you adopt the chosen method over other existing approaches.

You need to specify the approach you feel will be most appropriate for your research. Most postgraduate work involves empirical research. The successful completion of your work in the time allotted thus often depends on the ability to obtain the data needed. If your proposed research involves empirical work, you should provide an indication of the form and location of that empirical work and where and how you might collect any relevant data. You should give special attention to the feasibility of collecting the data. Generally, data acquisition techniques include direct approaches such as interviews and questionnaires, participant observations; indirect approaches such as instrumenting systems and fly on the wall; and independent approaches such as static and dynamic analysis and documentation analysis. Of these techniques, the first one is often not used in engineering, as most data are usually system generated.

Facilities Required

Remember to explain the facilities to be used for the research in your proposal. Usually, the list and description of the available facilities are available on the Web site of the department. If not all necessary facilities (hardware/software) required for your research project are available at the department, you should illustrate how they will be acquired and the time it may take to put everything in place. Do not go for the most expensive facilities when less expensive ones could be adapted and used for the same purpose. At the same time, you must think of an alternative in case your department may not be ready to purchase the quoted facilities in good time, which could in turn affect the completion time of your program.

Conclusion

Although no indication of the research findings can be presented at this stage, it is often beneficial to conclude the research proposal by indicating how you envisage the contribution that your research will make to debates and discussions in your particular subject area. This means providing an indication of the original contribution that you feel your research will make, suggesting how it may fill in gaps in the existing research, and showing how it may extend the understanding of particular topics. Conclusions should reflect the quality of your ideas as expressed in your writing.

List of Key References

Your references should provide the reader with a good sense of your grasp on the literature and how you can contribute to it. Be sure to reference the most recent texts and resources that you think will play a large role in your analysis. It should show critical reflection in the selection of appropriate texts and be used throughout your proposal to demonstrate that you have read and had a fair understanding of the work of others. Literature not cited in the text should not appear here and vice versa. It is also important to follow a particular standard formatting style in your proposal. The IEEE format is well known in engineering, and MLA and APA in humanity and social sciences.

(Adapted from M. F. Akorede & S. Amuda. 2014. Writing a Competitive Preliminary Research Proposal for an Engineering Ph.D. Degree. *IEEE Potentials,* 33(3):13–16. and E. A. Wents. 2014. *How to Design, Write, and Present a Successful Dissertation Proposal.* Los Angeles: Sage Publications.)

> **Tasks**

❶ Summarize the components of a research proposal based on the sample reading in a few keywords and fill in the table.

Components	Keywords
1)	

(Continued)

Components	Keywords
2)	
3)	
4)	
5)	
6)	
7)	

❷ Read the following pairs of topics and decide which is more suitable for a short-term research. The first one is given as an example.

No.	Topics	Suitable or Not
1)	a. In what way are graduate students of Southeast University (SEU) (dis)satisfied with their college life?	√
	b. Students' college life	
2)	a. Job prospect of M.S. graduates at SEU	
	b. An employment review	

(Continued)

No.	Topics	Suitable or Not
3)	a. India in the age of the Moguls	
	b. Royal monuments of India during the age of the Moguls	
4)	a. Classification of anxiety	
	b. Anxiety type among the SEU graduates	
5)	a. English word learning	
	b. Needs analysis of English word learning among SEU graduates	
6)	a. Faculty bilingualism	
	b. Is personal success of SEU faculty members correlated with bilingualism?	
7)	a. Is there an environmental impact on cities in South America during holidays?	
	b. Is the volume of rubbish produced during the carnival in Buenos Aires related to the economic revenue generated compared with normal weekends?	
8)	a. Is there an increase in waterborne disease in the three days following summer holidays compared with the three days following normal days in Caracas?	
	b. Is the water quality of South American cities with a large population worse on Christmas day than on normal days?	

❸ **Decide whether the following questions are appropriate for research topics. Why or why not? And how do you improve them if necessary?**

1) How many cars are there visiting the Desert Vista Mall?

_____

_____

2) How do we improve reading in elementary schools?

_____

_____

3) Can remote sensing be used to detect impervious surfaces?

_____

_____

III **Language Focus**

A. Personal Pronouns

	Singular	**Plural**
First person	I, me (my, mine)	we, us (our, ours)
Second person	you (your, yours)	you (your, yours)
Third person	she, her (her, hers) he, him (his) it (its) one (one's)	they, them (their, theirs)

- First person pronouns

You can strengthen your impersonal tone and establish credibility by removing first person pronouns in academic writing.

- Second person pronouns

Second person pronouns are seldom used in academic writing unless you give instructions.

- Third person pronouns

Third person pronouns sound more objective and convincing, so they are safer and more widely used in academic writing.

〉Tasks

❶ Rewrite the following sentences to make them more academic by avoiding first and second person pronouns.

1) I think that the methodology section is a hugely important part of your research proposal.

_____

_____

2) When you review literature, you should be aware that you need to identify existing gaps that your research intends to fill.

_____

_____

3) I chose this method because it was less complex.

_____

_____

4) My reading has shown that there are several reasons why plants are dispersed by ants.

_____

_____

5) The review of recent related literature could help you discover the latest facilities that are more efficient than earlier existing ones in carrying out your work.

_____

_____

6) I also found that the results of this study concurred with Berg's (1975) hypothesis that seeds are protected from fire through their burial in ants nests.

___

② **Rewrite the following paragraphs to make them more academic by avoiding first and second person pronouns.**

For our project we decided to check out the impact of two simple actions aimed at getting more female employees to use the stairs at a five-floor worksite. The first thing we did was that we put up a health sign that linked stair use to health and fitness. And the second thing was an e-mail which we asked the worksite doctor to send out. We asked him to point out how regular stair use could be really good for general fitness. We did the research by checking things out in four states: a baseline week, the week after the sign, the week after the e-mail and then three weeks after that.

We were really pleased that stair use went up a lot in the week after the sign, from a baseline of 69% to 77%, and then up again to 89% after the e-mail. Unfortunately, four weeks after the e-mail was sent out, stair use went down to 67% and we were very disappointed about that. We had expected these simple actions to lead to more stair use, but we didn't think the positive effect would've vanished after a month. So it's really difficult to make any recommendations based on our evidence.

___
___
___
___
___
___
___
___
___
___

B. Nominalization

The word "nominalization" defines itself, since it is itself an example of a nominalization. When you turn a verb or an adjective into a noun, you nominalize it, creating a nominalization. Nominalization types differ according to the level of organization at which the nominalization takes place. Three types of nominalizations can be distinguished: nominalizations at the level of the word (e.g. *reject, rejection*), nominalizations which nominalize a structure that lies in between a verb and an object (e.g. *Sam's rejection of the budget*) and finally, nominalizations consisting of full clauses (e.g. *Failure could result in rejection of the budget.*).

> **Tasks**

❶ Write down the noun form of the words in the following table.

Words	Noun Forms
discover	
refer	
special	
describe	
investigate	
propose	
indicate	

(Continued)

Words	Noun Forms
specific	
assume	
efficient	
liable	
duplicate	
extensive	
significant	
suffice	

❷ **Rewrite the following sentences to make them more academic by using nominalization.**

1) Many children experience worries when they go to school for the first time.

_____

_____

2) Crime was increasing rapidly and the police were becoming concerned.

_____

_____

3) Elephants argue over small concerns, just like humans.

_____

_____

4) We need to know which parts of our library are being used most extensively so that we can project what resources are most needed.

_____

_____

5) I know English well. I worked for three years in a factory in Shanghai. I think I am good enough for the job.

_____

_____

❸ **Rewrite the following paragraph to make it more academic by using nominalization.**

Because only a few people have most of the money and power in Australia, I conclude that it is not an equal society. Society has an upper, middle and lower class and I think that most people when they are born into one class, end up staying in that class for their whole life. When all three classes are looked at more closely, other things such as the differences between the sexes and people's racial backgrounds also add to the unequal nature of Australian society.

_____

_____

_____

_____

_____

_____

_____

Academic Writing Skills

In this book, you will not only acquire the knowledge of academic writing, but also writing skills; you will not only practice writing individual components of a paper, but also go through the whole process of doing your own research, based on which you will be able to produce a real research paper and make an oral presentation at the end of the semester as a learning outcome. Please go to Appendix 2 (on Pages 155–156) for a suggested schedule for a short-term research.

A. Selecting a Topic

Select a topic you really like, are curious about, or are an expert on. You are like a traveler who is choosing where to go. If it is a place you like, you'll enjoy getting there. But if it turns out to be somewhere you do not like, getting there would be a misery for you. So make sure that this topic is interesting to you.

❯ Task

The following is a list of topics that you may be interested in. Choose three topics and discuss whether they are suitable for your group project with your teammates. You can also propose your own.

Topics	Possibilities for Research
1) Students' living expenses	
2) English word learning	
3) Low-carbon life	

(Continued)

Topics	Possibilities for Research
4) Primary education in China	
5) Choosing a wife/husband	
6) Job prospect of students	
7) 5G	
8)	
9)	
10)	

B. Formulating the Focus

The generalized idea that you select as a research topic should be narrowed down and developed to a specifically defined written document and oral presentation. The topic starts where the area of specialization left off and digs deeper into those themes by refining what is known about your particular area, identifying the methods used to investigate those themes, and highlighting what remains unknown. So determiners or modifiers are usually added to the first version of the topic.

〉Task

Narrow down the three topics in the table on Pages 33–34 that you are most interested in by limiting them to some aspects, e.g., to a certain population, theoretical foundation or methodology.

1) _____

2) _____

3) _____

C. Establishing a Working Title

A working title is a title you initially think of in order to establish a focus for your research and writing. As you read and become more involved in the subject of your project, your viewpoint may change. For example, the following is James' working title and the process of refinement.

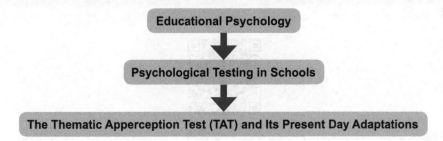

Task

The following is Eric's research topic. Fill in the blanks to show a possible process of refinement of his working title.

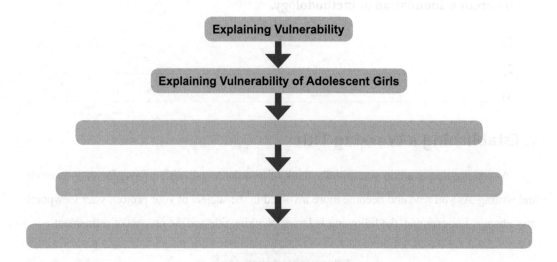

本章配套资源

UNIT 3
Introduction & Literature Review

Learning Objectives

- To understand the general functions of the introduction section;

- To learn how to cite other people's previous work;

- To get familiar with the writing of a literature review;

- To learn how to avoid plagiarism by paraphrasing.

A. Introduction

The introduction of a research paper is a summary or overview of your research for guiding your readers. A good introduction is obviously essential to the whole research paper, and therefore, knowing how to write the introduction is important to academic writing. Work in pairs or groups and discuss the following questions:

- What are the general functions of the introduction section?

- What do you think is the most important function of the introduction section?

- What are probably included in the introduction section?

B. Literature Review

A literature review is not simply a summary of what you have read, but a critical and in-depth evaluation of the previous research. It focuses on a specific topic of interest to you and includes a critical analysis of the relationship among different opinions, and then relates this review to the work of your own. It may be written as a stand-alone paper or to provide a theoretical framework and rationale for a research study so as to become a part of the introduction section, especially in term papers or journal articles. However, in a thesis or dissertation it will be an entire chapter. Work in pairs or groups and discuss the following questions:

- What is the purpose of writing a literature review?

- What steps may be taken in conducting a literature review?

- How do we cite other people's previous work in our own research articles?

Sample Reading

Sample 1

The Application of Swales' Model
in Writing a Research Article Introduction

Introduction

A research article is one of the genres of academic writing that is believed to be a great medium for spreading and disseminating knowledge in the academic world (Peacock, 2002). The need for information and knowledge from other experts from outside of one's local area has made research articles an important genre amongst scholars and researchers, who refer to the already-published research articles in writing a good research article in order to convince readers, editors as well as reviewers that the research article proposed deserves to be published (Flowerdew, 1999). The importance of research article development in academic communities has stimulated many scientists to conduct research on it, including the organization structure of research articles. As part of the interest of studies conducted on all sections of research articles, the introduction section has received special attention.

Writing a research article introduction is demanding. Safnil (2007) states that the introduction for a research article represents the connection between the readers and the authors' work, if it can bridge the gap between the knowledge of the intended readers and the research paper, then it will show that the introduction is successful. Hunston (1994) as cited in Safnil (2007) also claims that the introduction section communicates the subpersuasive purpose of the research article which shows that the research article is necessary and worthwhile. Thus, if readers find that the introduction to the article is convincing, interesting, and necessary, they will be more likely to read the whole article. Gupta (as cited in Safnil, 2007) asserts that writing an introduction for a scientific text raises problems for not only novice authors or students but also for professional or experienced authors. Additionally, Flowerdew (1999) states that "the introduction is challenging because it requires a persuasive style of writing in which the individual voice of the author(s) needs to come through".

On the basis of the importance, position, and function of a research article introduction, a standard schema is needed in order to write one successfully. Otherwise, the writers' intended purpose may not be successfully conveyed to the readers and the writers may fail to convince them and also reviewers as well as editors that the article proposed deserves to be published. This researcher, therefore, believes that the CARS or Swales' model is a good schema to use in writing a research article introduction. Based on the above research problem, the author formulated the following research question: How does the Swales' model apply for writing the introduction section to convey the essence of a research article?

The present study tries to look at the application of the Swales' model in providing a solution for the problems faced by scholars and researchers in organizing an introduction section for a research article. In particular, it aims to find out how the Swales' model is applicable for conveying the proper message for the introduction section to a research article. Referring to the context of the author of this study, the study of the development of a research article in English is still limited in undergraduate and graduate level studies. Moreover, it is found that hardly any studies have been conducted on the application of the Swales' model. Thus, the result of this study will be fruitful for students at undergraduate and graduate levels in writing a research article in English. It is hoped that this kind of study may contribute to teaching academic writing and help teachers and students in organizing academic articles in English.

(Adapted from Burhanuddin Yasin & Hijjatul Qamariah. 2014. The Application of Swales' Model in Writing a Research Article Introduction. *Studies in English Language and Education*, 1(1): 29–41.)

Sample 2

Poverty and Environmental Degradation:
A Review and Analysis of the Nexus

Introduction

The poor have traditionally taken the brunt of the blame for causing society's many problems including, more recently, environmental degradation. There seems to be a general consensus that poverty is a major cause of environmental degradation. For example, in one of the conclusions of the Bruntland Commission Report, which incidentally has been accepted as the blueprint for environmental conservation, it is explicitly stated that poverty is a major cause of environmental problems and amelioration of poverty is a necessary and central condition of any effective program addressing the environmental concerns. Along similar lines, Jalal (1993), the Asian Development Bank's chief of the environment department argues, "it is generally accepted that environmental degradation, rapid population growth, and stagnant production are closely linked with the fast spread of acute poverty in many countries of Asia". The World Bank (1992) joined the consensus with its World Development Report, where it explicitly states, "poor families who have to meet short-term needs mine the natural capital by excessive cutting of trees for firewood and failure to replace soil nutrients".

However, there has been a rising trend in the economic literature which disputes the conventional theory and argues that simple generalizations of this multi-dimensional problem are often erroneous and miss many important points and that a more complex set of variables comes into play (Leach and Mearns, 1995). These studies point out demographic, cultural, and institutional factors as important variables in the poverty-environmental degradation nexus. An intricate web of factors plus feedback loops from environmental degradation to poverty makes the process of identifying causality links, if any, between environmental degradation and poverty a difficult exercise. However, these studies have been few and isolated and it is interesting to note that until recently, there has been very little in-depth coordinated empirical research in the economics of environmental degradation-poverty causality relationships.

Both poverty and environmental degradation have been increasing in many developing countries; hence there is a pressing need first to evaluate and analyze the poverty-environmental degradation nexus, and second, to prescribe policy options to mitigate or eradicate these two problems. The primary objective of the paper is to analyze critically the existing literature on the poverty-environmental degradation nexus and try to make "some order out of the chaos" inherent in this complex and difficult subject.

For this paper, the analysis is limited to the following four main natural resources which are under serious threat of degradation in many developing countries: i) forests; ii) land; iii) water; and iv) air. Biodiversity is excluded at this point because the preliminary literature search found only scattered and limited information which was too crude to contribute to the analysis of the poverty-environmental degradation link. However, it should not be inferred that biodiversity is less important than any of the four resources investigated; indeed, it is an area which needs particular attention in the future. The paper concludes with a summary of the main findings of the literature review together with suggestions for future research.

(Adapted from Anantha K. Duraiappah. 1998. Poverty and Environmental Degradation: A Review and Analysis of the Nexus. *World Development*, 26(12): 2169–2179.)

> **Tasks**

❶ Read Sample 1 and decide what elements this sample includes and how they function.

Paragraphs	Elements	Functions
1		
2		
3		
4		

❷ Read Sample 2 and decide what elements this sample includes and how they function.

Paragraphs	Elements	Functions
1		
2		
3		
4		

Ⅲ Language Focus

A. Tenses in Citation

- Simple present tense

Authors mostly use the simple present tense verbs to cite other authors' ideas, relate what other authors say or discuss the literature, theoretical concepts, methods, etc. For example:

- When it comes to technology, King *states* that we "need to be comfortable enough with technology tools and services so that we can help point our patrons in the right direction, even if we aren't intimately familiar with how the device works" (11).

- Simple past tense

When you use the past tense, the reporting verb often occurs as an integral citation. In other words, citations with past tense verbs and named researchers as subject seem to have the discourse role of providing particulars for recounting events, results found or a preceding generalization, or the basis for a claim, etc. Common verbs in the past tense are *investigated*, *studied*, *compared*, *analyzed*, *found*, and *examined*. In the example below, the citation reports the results of a single study.

- Carlson and Benton (2007) *found* that as they increased the participants' stress levels, the results of their performance deteriorated.

- Present perfect tense

The present perfect tense can be used to state that the research results are recent, expressing what has been found over an extended period in the past and up to the present to highlight the direct relevance of previous studies to the writer's own research. For example:

- Although the results of pervious studies showed that further research was warranted in this area, recent studies *have demonstrated* that educational methodology is now moving in a new direction (Jones, 2007; Karstal, 2008).

Check Sample 2 and complete the following table.

Questions	Answers	Purposes
1) Are there any sentences written in the present tense?		
2) Are there any sentences written in the past tense?		
3) Are there any sentences written in the present perfect tense?		
4) Which tense is used more? Why do you think this is the case?		

B. Citing Verbs

In academic writing, it is often necessary to refer to the research of others and to report on their findings. In order to do so, we have to use citing verbs. Words like "say" and "tell" are normally used in oral conversations, but they are not appropriate in formal academic writing.

Citing verbs differ in terms of their strength; for example, "suggest" is much weaker and more tentative than "argue". The two verbs convey very different pictures about how the author you are studying sees his or her materials and research.

Some citing verbs are used principally to show what the writer does and does not do. These verbs do not indicate any value judgment on the part of the writer; they are called "neutral" citing verbs.

A second group of verbs is used to show that the writer has an inclination to believe something but still wishes to be hesitant; we call these "tentative" citing verbs.

Finally, if the writer has strong arguments to put forward and is absolutely sure of his or her ground, we can use "strong" citing verbs to refer to these ideas.

The main citing verbs in English are classified in terms of their function and strength as follows:

"Neutral" Citing Verbs	"Tentative" Citing Verbs	"Strong" Citing Verbs
describe; show; reveal; study; demonstrate; note; point out; indicate; report; observe; assume; take into consideration; examine; state; believe (unless this is a strong belief); mention	suggest; speculate; intimate; hypothesize; moot; imply; propose; recommend; posit the view that; question the view that; postulate	argue; claim; emphasize; contend; maintain; assert; theorize; support the view that; deny; negate; refute; reject; challenge; strongly believe that; counter the view/argument that

When citing verbs are used, the structure of sentences can vary and be flexible. For example:

- Jones (1999) argues, in his study of thermodynamics, that...

- As Jones (1999) argues in his study of thermodynamics, ...

- In his study of thermodynamics, Jones (1999) argues that...

It is possible (and often quite attractive stylistically) to invert the subject and verb when citing. For example:

- Thermodynamics, argues Jones (1999), is...

Citing the work of others often needs an extra sentence introduction or "lead-in". For example:

- In considering Smith's discussion on thermodynamics, Jones (1999) argues that...

> **Task**

Read the following three extracts on the issue of poverty and crime. Use appropriate verbs to cite the underlined opinions and then integrate the extracts into one paragraph as part of a literature review.

1) A study by McClatchy Newspapers, released in March finds that the ranks of the severely impoverished are rapidly escalating. <u>The study found that the percentage of</u>

poor Americans who are living in extreme poverty has reached a 32-year high. Today nearly 16 million Americans live in "deep or severe poverty". This is defined as individuals living at half of the federal poverty line. This drastic rise in the level of poverty extends beyond the traditional ghetto and reaches to suburban and rural communities. At the same time, the poverty rise creates severe social problems. (By Joseph Williams, 2010)

2) Starting from the 1970s, studies in the U.S. pointed more and more at the link between unemployment, poverty, and crime. After that, other connections with income level, schooling, neighborhood quality, education, etc. were revealed as well. Fresh research from the U.K. even indicates that economic cycles may affect variations in property and violent crimes. But most important of all, the unmistakable characteristic of poverty and crime is that they're both geographically concentrated in the same areas. In other words, where you find poverty is also where you find crime. And this reveals the strong connection between the two issues. (By Carl Holmes, 2011)

3) Sociologist and criminal justice scholars have found a direct correlation between poverty and crime. One economic theory of crime assumes that people weigh the consequences of committing crime. They resort to crime only if the cost or consequences are outweighed by the potential benefits to be gained. The logical conclusion to this theory is that people living in poverty are far more likely to commit property crimes such as burglary, larceny, or theft. (By David Garland, 2012)

IV Academic Writing Skills

A. Citing Previous Research

In any research paper, you will use information from other sources, placing your research project in the context of previous findings in the field, and it is essential to use in-text citations to accredit other researchers.

The exact format of an in-text citation will depend on the style you need to use, for example, APA. Check with your academic institution to ensure that you provide the in-text citations in the format that they are expecting.

When you cite the work of other authors, you may choose to focus either on the information provided by that author, or on the author him- or herself. The first focus is called information prominent because the information is given primary importance. In the second type, author prominent citation, the author's name is given more emphasis. It serves as the subject of the sentence, followed by the year in parentheses, and then by the information. Such citations can be either strong or weak, depending on how much emphasis is placed on the identity of the author. For example:

- **Information prominent citation:** Shrinking markets are also evident in other areas. The wool industry is experiencing difficulties related to falling demand worldwide since the development of high-quality synthetic fibers (Smith, 2000).

- **Author prominent citation:** Shrinking markets are also evident in other areas. As Smith (2000) pointed out, the wool industry was experiencing difficulties related to falling demand worldwide since the development of high-quality synthetic fibers. However, Jones et al. (2004) found that industry difficulties were more related to quality of supply than to demand issues. It is clear that considerable disagreement exists about the underlying sources of these problems.

- **Weak author prominent citation:** Several authors have reported that the wool industry is experiencing difficulties related to falling demand since the development of high-quality synthetic fibers (Nguyen, 2005; Smith, 2000; Wilson, 2003).

Task

Read the following sentences and decide which kind of citation is used. Then rewrite them in another kind of citation.

1) Several authors have suggested that automated testing should be more readily accepted (Balcer, 1989; Stahl, 1989; Carver and Tai, 1991).

_____

_____

2) For viscoelastic fluids, the behavior of the time-dependent stresses in the transient shear flows is also very important (Boger et al., 1994).

_____

_____

3) Close (1983) developed a simplified theory using an analogy between heat and mass transfer and the equivalent heat transfer only case.

_____

_____

B. Relating Literature to Your Research

A literature review is a report or overview of literature found relevant to an area of research or study. It provides an overview of the current literature that is available on a given subject, usually in academia. A literature review should answer the following questions:

- What do we already know in the immediate area concerned?
- What are the characteristics of the key concepts or the main factors or variables?
- What are the relationships between these key concepts, factors or variables?
- What are the existing theories?
- Where are the inconsistencies or other shortcomings in our knowledge and understanding?
- What views need to be (further) tested?
- What evidence is lacking, inconclusive, contradictory or too limited?
- Why should we (further) study the research problem?
- What contribution can the present study be expected to make?

- What research designs or methods seem unsatisfactory?

It is easy to write a bad literature review and difficult to write a good one. The main mistake that a lot of people make is to write a literature review that looks like this:

■ Until recently many researchers have shown interest in the field of coastal erosion and the resulting beach profiles. They have carried out numerous laboratory experiments and field observations to illuminate the darkness of this field. Their findings and suggestions are reviewed here.

Jachowski (2008) developed a model investigation conducted on the interlocking precast concrete block seawall. After a result of a survey of damages caused by the severe storm at the coast of U.S.A., a new and specially shaped concrete block was developed for use in shore protection. This block was designed to be used in a revetment type seawall that would be both durable and economical as well as reduce wave run-up and overtopping, and scour at its base or toe. It was proved that effective shore protection could be designed utilizing these units.

Hom-Ma and Horikawa (2008) studied waves forces acting on the seawall which was located inside the surf zone. On the basis of the experimental results conducted to measure waves forces against a vertical wall, the authors proposed an empirical formula of wave pressure distribution on a seawall. The computed results obtained by using the above formula were compared well with the field data of wave pressure on a vertical wall.

Selezov and Zheleznyak (2009) conducted experiments on scour of sea bottom in front of harbor seawalls, on the basis of the theoretical investigation of solitary wave interaction with a vertical wall using Boussinesque type equation. It showed that the numerical results were in reasonable agreement with laboratory experimental data.

❯ Task

Consider again the purpose of writing a literature review. Then answer the following questions about the literature review above.

1) What questions does this literature review answer?

_____

_____

_____

2)   What questions doesn't it answer?

_____

_____

_____

3)   Which method has the writer used to organize the literature review?

_____

_____

_____

4)   Is it a good literature review? Why or why not?

_____

_____

_____

C. Avoiding Plagiarism

Plagiarism is copying or borrowing another person's ideas or words without proper citing. Using another author's intellectual property without permission is thought to be an academic dishonesty. However, it doesn't mean that we should not use the writings of other authors. We can include other authors' ideas or words in our own papers by quoting, paraphrasing or summarizing and citing the sources.

When paraphrasing, we should modify not only the vocabulary of the passage but also the method of expression. We should use synonyms to replace all the words we can except generic words. Besides, we should change the structure of sentences: change the sentence pattern, choose different parts of speech, or change the voice.

Summarizing is another way to avoid plagiarism. The main difference between paraphrasing and summarizing is the size of the eventual result: A summary is much shorter than an original passage while a paraphrase is almost as long as or even longer than the original passage. For example:

- **Original sentence:** The fox stalked its prey in the moonlight, its large ears and bright eyes on high alert for the rabbit's next move.

- **A paraphrase:** The rabbit stayed still in the light of the moon while the fox surveyed the land using its spectacular hearing and night vision.

- **A summary:** Foxes hunt rabbits at night using their ears and eyes.

> Tasks

❶ **Read the following original sentence and the three paraphrases. Then decide which paraphrase is acceptable and which is unacceptable. Give reasons.**

Original sentence: We do not yet understand all the ways in which brain chemicals are related to emotions and thoughts, but the salient point is that our state of mind has an immediate and direct effect on our state of body. (Source: Siegel, B. 1986. *Love, Medicine and Miracles*. New York: Harper and Row.)

Paraphrase 1: Siegel (1986) writes that although the relationship between brain chemistry and thoughts and feelings is not fully understood, we do know that our psychological state affects our physical state.

_____

_____

_____

Paraphrase 2: Siegel (1986) writes that we still do not know all the ways in which brain chemistry is related to emotions and thoughts, but the important point is that our mental state has an immediate and direct effect on our physical state.

_____

_____

_____

Paraphrase 3: According to Siegel (1986), our mind affects our body quickly and directly, although we do not yet understand every aspect of how brain chemicals relate to emotions and thoughts.

_____

_____

_____

❷ Paraphrase the following sentences to make them more academic.

1) The bomb exploded and caused many casualties.

_____

_____

2) Among all the feelings of mankind, love is probably the noblest.

_____

_____

3) With no doubt, these firms are doing their part in educating the next generation of thinkers.

_____

_____

4) No one knows how many CEOs suffer from alcoholism and drug abuse, but estimates run as high as 30%.

_____

_____

5) European leaders generally agree that if European countries would unify, there would be a more stable economy.

_____

_____

_____

6) Attitudes toward the elderly are changing dramatically as baby boomers grow older. For many years the elderly were seen as less useful once they reached retirement age. However, the new research points to the increased productivity of aged workers, even those who are in their 80s and 90s.

_____

_____

_____

_____

D. Writing a Literature Review

Writing a literature review is often the most daunting part of writing an article, book, thesis, or dissertation. In their book, *Destination Dissertation: A Traveler's Guide to a Done Dissertation*, Sonja Foss and William Walters describe a highly efficient and effective way of writing a literature review. Below is a summary of the steps they outline as well as a step-by-step method for writing a literature review.

- **Step 1:** Decide on your areas of research.

Before you begin to search for articles or books, decide beforehand what areas you are going to research. Make sure that you only get articles and books in those areas, even if you come across fascinating books in other areas.

- **Step 2:** Search for the literature.

Conduct a comprehensive bibliographic search of books and articles in your area of research.

- **Step 3:** Find relevant excerpts in the books and articles.

Skim the contents of each book and article and look specifically for these five things: claims, conclusions, and findings about the constructs you are investigating; definitions of terms; calls for follow-up studies relevant to your project; gaps you notice in the literature; and disagreement about the constructs you are investigating.

Make sure to note the name of the author and the page number following each excerpt. Do this for each article and book that you have in your stack of literature.

- **Step 4:** Encode the literature.

Sort the excerpts into similar topics. Figure out what the main themes are. Place each excerpt into a themed file. Make sure each note goes into a file.

- **Step 5:** Create your conceptual schema.

Figure out the best way to organize the excerpts that make sense.

- **Step 6:** Write your literature review.

Use that conceptual schema to write up your literature review based on the excerpts. Don't forget to include the citations as you write, so as not to lose track of who said what.

Once you complete these six steps, you will have a complete draft of your literature review.

Follow the six steps on the previous page to write a literature review for your research article.

本章配套资源

UNIT 4
Methodology Description

 Learning Objectives

- To learn to describe research methodology;

- To understand the importance of passive voice in academic writing;

- To make proper use of sequential markers in writing a process;

- To acquire the skills of designing a questionnaire.

In natural sciences the method section is often called Materials and Methods. In social sciences it is common to introduce a section called Theory and Methods. Sometimes it is divided into two sections: Theoretical Framework and Methods.

Research methodology is mainly concerned with the answers to the following questions:

- Why is a particular research undertaken?
- How has one formulated a research question?
- What types of data have been collected?
- What particular methods have been used?
- Why is a particular technique of data analysis used?

The following terms are vital in describing your methodology.

Research methodology: Research methodology describes the method which the researchers will use in gathering relevant data for their research work and deciding the instrument needed for the data collection, the measure taken to ensure that the instrument would achieve the intended result, and the techniques employed in data analysis.

Data collection: A good research is not likely to be achieved without the collection and analysis of data. The collected and analyzed data determines the result of the research. If the wrong data is collected or the process of data collection is not the right one for the intended research, the analysis will be faulty and that will bring about a wrong result. It is the responsibility of the researchers to ensure that they make use of relevant data and valued instrument for data collection and analysis. Data can be primary or secondary.

Quantitative data: This kind of data deals with quantities, values, or numbers. Thus, it is usually expressed in numerical forms, such as length, size, amount, price, and even duration. The use of statistics to generate and subsequently analyze this type of data adds credibility to research, so quantitative data is generally seen as more reliable and objective.

Qualitative data: This type of data, on the other hand, deals with quality, so that it is descriptive rather than numerical in nature. Unlike quantitative data, it is generally unmeasurable, and is gained mostly through observation. Researchers often make use of adjectives and other descriptive words to refer to data on appearance, color, texture, and other qualities.

Sample Reading

Parental Phenol Exposure and Spontaneous Abortion in Chinese Population Residing in the Lower Reach of the Yangtze River

Methodology

The subjects were volunteers from affiliated hospitals of Nanjing Medical University. The Institutional Review Board of Nanjing Medical University approved the protocol. All the studies involving human subjects were conducted under full compliance with government policies and the Helsinki Declaration. After explanation of the study procedures and clarification of questions raised, all subjects signed informed consent forms. A complete physical examination, including height and weight, was performed. A questionnaire was designed to collect information, including personal background, lifestyle factors, occupational and environmental exposures, genetic risk factors, sexual and reproduction status, medical history, and physical activity. The controls included were couples who had no history of spontaneous abortion and had at least one living child. The cases were couples who suffered a medically unexplained spontaneous abortion. We excluded the subjects with some known factors related to spontaneous abortion, such as chromosomal abnormality, uterine abnormalities, autoimmune diseases, infection, occupational exposure to some toxins suspected to be associated with spontaneous abortion from this study. 295 eligible couples were recruited to participate. Of the approached, 84.7% consented (250 couples: 70 couples eligible cases and 180 couples eligible controls). All participants claimed that their lifestyles and environments had not changed for several months leading up to sample collection. Urine samples were collected from each subject on the designated morning. Urine samples were frozen at $-20\,^{\circ}\text{C}$ for phenol analysis.

The total urinary concentrations of phenols were measured with a previously described method using ultra-high performance liquid chromatography. Firstly, urine samples were incubated in 1 ml ammonium acetate buffer solution for hydrolyzation with β-glucuronidase overnight. After hydrolysis, the phenols were extracted and preconcentrated with solid phase extraction (SPE) and determined with UPLC electro-spray ionization (negative ion mode)-MS/MS. The intra- and inter-day precisions for these compounds were between 2% and 41% and the recoveries were between 86% and 131% at spiked concentration of 220 ng/ml. Quality control samples were analyzed in parallel with unknown samples in each analytical series. Creatinine (CR) concentrations were analyzed for correcting the phenol concentration variations caused by fluctuated urine concentration and dilution. CR concentrations of urine were measured with an automated chemistry analyzer (7020 Hitachi, Japan).

All data analysis was performed by using Stata 9.2 statistical software package (Stata Corp, LP). T-test was used to compare the mean age, body mass index (BMI) between case and control groups. The chi-square test was used to evaluate the differences in smoking status and drinking status between case and control groups. All samples were divided into two groups for statistical analysis. The samples with concentrations<LOD were assigned to the low exposure group, and the remaining samples with detectable concentrations were assigned to the high exposure group. Odds ratios (ORs) with 95% confidence intervals (CIs) were calculated for spontaneous abortion in relation to urine phenol exposure by paternal smoking, maternal alcohol use and BMI which were significantly different between case and control groups. In addition, urinary creatinine was included as a continuous variable to adjust for urinary dilution. We considered $p \leqslant 0.05$ statistically significant.

(Adapted from Chen, X. J. et al. 2013. Parental Phenol Exposure and Spontaneous Abortion in Chinese Population Residing in the Lower Reach of the Yangtze River. *Chemosphere,* 93: 217–222.)

> Tasks

❶ **What information elements does this method section include? Fill in the following table with relevant details from the sample reading.**

Information Elements	Relevant Details

(Continued)

Information Elements	Relevant Details

② **Answer the following questions based on the sample reading.**

1) How was the sample collected?

_____

_____

2) Is the sample size big enough to be representative of the study population? Why?

_____

_____

3) What is the questionnaire designed for in this survey?

_____

_____

III Language Focus

A. The Passive Voice

The passive voice is widely used in academic writing, because passive structures have less subjective coloring in most cases than active ones. When you describe a process or a scientific experiment, it is important to write in a neutral style, as an observer. To do this, you can use the passive voice. There are three instances in which the passive voice is recommended: i) when you do not know or do not care about who has performed the action; ii) when you focus on the receiver instead of the performer of the action; and iii) when you would like to remain in a neutral or objective position in writing. Some examples from the methodology section using passive structures are as follows:

- The study *was conducted* at the beginning of the semester and the final one *was given* at the end of the semester. (procedure)

- In summer, the greenhouse *was cooled* by pulling in air through water saturated pads on the south end of the building. (specially designed material)

- The quartz reactors tested for this work *are fabricated* by the A & B Sales Company of Wheeling, Leeds, U.K. (instrument)

- In order to provide a broad sampling of college students, respondents *were recruited* from diverse fields of study. (sampling)

- The final scores *were computed* into mean averages (X) and standard deviations (SD). (data analysis)

> **Tasks**

1 **Reread the sample reading and write down the verbs using the passive voice in the following table.**

Information Elements	Verbs Using the Passive Voice
Sample collection	
Procedure	
Materials	
Data analysis	

❷ **Rewrite the following paragraph by using the passive voice to make it more academically acceptable.**

Some people consider a poison ivy infection to be humorous. But it is not funny at all. Contact with the plant causes a rash that has the intensity of a fresh mosquito bite and lasts for several days. Scientists have studied poison ivy infection for centuries, but they have found no preventive pill or inoculation. The poisonous substance in the plant is called urushiol. After urushiol has touched the skin, blisters and weeping sores will soon cover the exposed area.

_____

_____

_____

_____

_____

❸ **The following expressions in the table are commonly used in the method section. Complete the paragraph below by translating the Chinese in the brackets into English.**

Subjects/Participants	choose; include; recruit; select; volunteer; participate...
Materials	be composed of; be located; be installed; be equipped with; obtain; supply...
Procedure	conduct; implement; administer; perform...
Data analysis	be determined; be scored; be conducted; be used; be performed; be calculated...

A group of MBA candidates from Southeast University were recruited as participants for the investigation. 1)_____(问卷调查被实施) after the topic of the BSC had been discussed in the course. 136 students enrolled in a managerial accounting course 2)_____ (完成了此次问卷).

3)_____

（表 2 给出了这些参与者的背景信息）. As is shown, the majority of the participants were girl students. 4)_____

_____（参与者的平均年龄约 29 岁）, 5)_____

_____（平均工作年限约 6 年）. The average number of accounting courses was approximately four for each semester.

❹ **The following sentences are taken from the method section of different research articles. Polish or correct them so that they are more academically acceptable.**

1) Table 5 shows the number of students per level and their L1 language backgrounds which are represented.

_____

_____

2) Two questionnaires which were sent respectively to the personnel officers and business employees show a similar result in terms of their perception of the use of English in their firm.

_____

_____

3) The scores of the two raters were averaged and all the data were entered for statistical analysis.

_____

_____

4) The model which was used in the experiment was a modified version of the 2009 Test package, which was originally developed by the Morrison Research Institute.

_____

_____

5) These engines used to be started by hand. Now we start them by electricity.

_____

_____

6) One of the great advantages of atomic power stations is the fact that people can build them in the very region where power is inadequate.

_____

_____

7) Observations are made daily at two hundred weather stations in and around the British Isles, which send in reports every three hours. Weather ships also make measurements of wind speed, temperature and pressure in the Atlantic.

_____

_____

8) People fix a kind of lid to the top of the pipe, and they allow the oil to flow out gently through taps.

_____

_____

B. Sequential Markers

A process paragraph explains how to do something or how something works. Process paragraphs are usually developed step by step in a chronological or logical sequence. The following sequencing expressions are more frequently used to link steps in a description of a process or to divide a process into steps:

- Firstly..., To begin with..., First of all..., etc.;
- Secondly..., Next..., After that..., In addition..., etc.;
- Finally..., Lastly..., etc.

> Task

The following sentences describe the process of making paper. Use sequential expressions to rewrite them into a cohesive paragraph.

1) The logs are placed in the shredder.

2) They are cut into small chips and mixed with water and acid.

3) They are heated and crushed to a heavy pulp which is cleaned.

4) It is chemically bleached to whiten it.

5) It is passed through rollers to flatten it.

6) Sheets of wet paper are produced.

7) The water is removed from the sheets which are pressed, dried, and refined, and the finished paper is produced.

_____

_____

_____

_____

_____

Academic Writing Skills

A. Identifying Information Elements

A well-organized, logically ordered and understandable method section can make your paper or thesis a really outstanding work. Normally, a method section includes the following information elements:

- Overview of the research: a brief description about what has been done;

- Subjects: the people/subjects studied, or the things tested;

- Location: where a research takes place;

- Restrictions/Limiting conditions: precautions taken to make sure that the data is valid;

- Sampling techniques: describing how the subjects are selected for research;

- Materials: the materials used to conduct a study or an experiment;

- Procedure: the steps of conducting the research in a chronological order;

- Statistical treatment: describing how the statistics are examined.

Of all the information elements mentioned above, the only items that are always included in the method section are *materials* and *procedure*.

The following sentences are taken from the method section of different research articles. Write down the information element(s) presented.

1) A total of 369 participants of European origins (52.7% female) with a mean age of 27.2 years were recruited by research assistants in public places in the Montreal region.

   _____

   _____

2) The data used for the current analysis consists of 60 texts taken from 20 engineering journals.

   _____

   _____

3) Experimenters approached potential participants by introducing themselves as students from the University of Quebec in Montreal and then asked if they would agree to participate in a short study on facial expressions.

   _____

   _____

4) The study aims to examine the use of SEF as a tool for providing evidence of teaching effectiveness in tertiary education.

   _____

   _____

5) The results of the two questionnaires were subjected to statistical tests of reliability and significance using SPSS.

   _____

   _____

6) Envelopes containing the survey materials were sent to the local business manager of each union. In the envelopes, there was a cover letter explaining the project, the questionnaire itself, and a pre-paid return envelope. The union business manager was contacted and asked to select workers from his union and to send the envelopes to the

chosen workers.

7) The participants were 90 first-year students from the School of Foreign Languages at a key university in Nanjing. Their average age was 18 years old. They constituted a convenience sample.

8) The investigation was performed in a national laboratory affiliated to a research center for industrial automation in Nanjing, Jiangsu Province.

B. Ordering Methodology Elements

Essentially, the procedures by which researchers go about their work of describing, explaining, and predicting phenomena are called research methodology. You need to state the purpose of the study and define the problem/issue clearly. This guides you in deciding the methodology of research which involves:

- identifying the method of research;
- specifying the subjects of study;
- selecting an adequate representative sample of subjects;
- selecting reliable instruments for measuring the variables in a problem;
- selecting a research design and describing the procedure to be employed for conducting your research;
- collecting data;
- analyzing and interpreting your results.

Task

The following sentences are taken from the method section of a research article in a scrambled order. Try to put them back into a logical order. Write the sequential number in the box on the right side of the table below.

a. The data was rank-ordered from the lowest X value of 1.2 to the highest of 3.8—see Table 2 below.	
b. The SD scores show to what extent the teachers agreed among themselves when judging the gravity of each error.	
c. The survey was conducted by means of a questionnaire, in which the errors appeared in a random order.	
d. The assessors were instructed to view each error in its context and determine to what extent it deviated from normal English.	
e. The questionnaire included the context in which each error had occurred and a marking scale ranging from 0 for "no error" to 5 for "the most severe error".	
f. After scoring, the assessors were given the option to write down the principles that guided them in their scoring.	
g. The scores were computed into mean averages (X) and standard deviations (SD).	
h. Unless otherwise indicated, the numerical data in the text refers to the mean average scores.	
i. The higher the SD score, the more diverse the assessors' opinions regarding the gravity of the item.	

C. Gathering Information for a Method Section

The method section of a research paper provides the information by which a study's validity is judged. So it requires a clear and precise description of how an experiment was done, and the rationale for why specific experimental procedures were chosen. Therefore, the method section should describe:

- the materials used in the study;
- how the materials were prepared for the study;
- the research protocol;
- how measurements were made and what calculations were performed;
- which statistical tests were done to analyze the data.

> **Task**

Suppose you are required to write the method section of a research paper about a group of students' attendance in English class. The necessary information elements have been given in the table below. Gather information for your research and fill in the blanks of the table.

Research objective	To investigate into the status quo of a group of students' attendance in English class and reasons for their absence.
Subjects	
Sampling	
Materials	
Procedure	
Data analysis	

D. Describing Methodology

Although there is no standard way of writing the research methodology, a well-organized, logically ordered and easily understandable chapter on methodology makes your paper a really outstanding work. For the benefit of those who wonder how to write research methodology, a few tips are provided below. The methodology need not be described in detail, but it has to be justified so that the results have a validity and credibility.

- The selection between qualitative and quantitative research has to be justified.

- If a survey of students in five high schools in an area is selected, the sample size and the selection of samples have to be justified. Selection methods also have to be stated.

- Arrangements for data collection have to be stated and justified.

- Interview questions or questionnaires have to be stated and justified.

- Methods and software for analyzing data have to be stated and justified.

⟩Tasks

According to the information in the following table, write the method section of a research paper about an experiment to investigate into students' preferences and attitudes towards sugar-sweetened and artificially-sweetened beverages.

Research objective	To determine students' preferences and attitudes towards sugar-sweetened and artificially-sweetened beverages.
Subjects	10 participants, including 5 male students and 5 female students, from a Science English class, chosen at random.
Materials	30 straws, 2 cups, 1 blindfold, and 2 containers of Kool-Aid (a popular drink in the United States), 1 container with 4 cups of orange Kool-Aid sweetened with one half cup of sugar, the other container with 4 cups of orange Kool-Aid sweetened with 9 packets of NutraSweet brand artificial sweetener.

Procedure	10 volunteer students, in two lines, one for males and the other for females. Alternately, men and women test, with a blindfold over the eyes of the tester, he/she could not see; the two cups were filled with beverage, one with artificially-sweetened Kool-Aid and the other with sugar-sweetened Kool-Aid. Finally the remaining drink was thrown away, and the next tester came forward and repeated the process.
Data analysis	The final answers were tabulated for data analysis.

E. Designing a Questionnaire

The design of a questionnaire depends on whether the researcher wishes to collect qualitative information (i.e., exploratory information for a better understanding of something or for the generation of hypotheses on a subject) or quantitative information (to test specific hypotheses that have been generated previously).

A good questionnaire is one that: i) enables you to collect accurate data effectively; ii) facilitates data collecting, data processing, and data tabulating; iii) ensures that there is no collection of non-essential information; and iv) permits comprehensive and meaningful analysis as well as purposeful utilization of the data collected.

There are many different types of questions you can use to get the information that you need. In general, they fall into open and closed questions. An open question allows the respondents to use their own words to answer; for example, "What do you think are the main causes of racism?" A closed question gives respondents pre-defined options; for example, "Which of the following do you think is the main cause of racism: a, b, c, or d?"

The features of both open and closed questions are listed in the following table:

Features of Open Questions	Features of Closed Questions
Eliciting "rich" qualitative data	Eliciting quantitative data
Encouraging thought and freedom of expressions	Encouraging "mindless" replies
Discouraging responses from less literate respondents	Easy for respondents at any literacy level
Taking longer to answer and may put some people off	Quick to answer and may improve the response rate
More difficult to analyze—responses can be misinterpreted	Easy to "code" and analyze

Look closely at the following example of a rating scale in a questionnaire:

Do you agree or disagree that this company has the following:					
	Totally Agree	Partly Agree	Not Sure	Disagree	Totally Disagree
A good vacation policy	☐ 1	☐ 2	☐ 3	☐ 4	☐ 5
Good management feedback	☐ 1	☐ 2	☐ 3	☐ 4	☐ 5
Good medical insurance	☐ 1	☐ 2	☐ 3	☐ 4	☐ 5
Satisfying salary	☐ 1	☐ 2	☐ 3	☐ 4	☐ 5

Or, please rate the quality of the medical insurance in this company.

☐ Very Poor ☐ Poor ☐ Fair ☐ Good ☐ Very Good

The following are eight steps involved in designing a questionnaire:

- Determine the information required;
- Define the target respondents;
- Choose the method(s) of reaching your target respondents;
- Design questions;
- Put questions into a meaningful order and format;
- Check the length of the questionnaire;
- Pre-test the questionnaire;
- Develop the final survey form.

❯ Task

Work in groups of four and design a questionnaire to obtain information about students' class attendance and the reasons for their absence.

本章配套资源

UNIT 5
Results & Discussion

- To understand the major functions and elements of the results and discussion section;

- To learn how to describe graphic information;

- To grasp the tips for making comparison and contrast;

- To learn how to present the cause-and-effect relationship;

- To learn how to strengthen or weaken a claim.

I Warm-up

In a journal paper, the results and discussion section is to present the results with texts and the statistical techniques such as tables and graphs and then to explain and contemplate the results. The results section can be arranged according to the research questions, or the research methods. The discussion section part can either be a part of the results section or a separate section of its own, which should be in line with the practice of your target journal. The discussion section will always be connected to the introduction section by way of the question(s) or posed hypotheses and cited literature, but it does not simply repeat or rearrange the introduction section. Instead, it tells how your study has moved forward from where you leave us at the end of the introduction section.

Think about the following questions and then have a discussion with your classmates:

- What are the major functions of the results and discussion section?

- What major elements should be included in the results and discussion section?

- How do you describe graphic information in the results section?

- How do you compare and contrast the data presented in the graphs?

- How do you present a cause-and-effect relationship?

- How do you strengthen or weaken the claims?

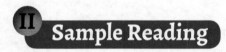

II Sample Reading

The Role of Language for Thinking and Task Selection in EFL Learners' Oral Collocational Production

Results

Types of Language for Thinking and Lexical Collocational Errors

One key issue in this study was whether a learner's type of language for thinking influences lexical collocational production. We explored this issue by examining one retrospective report on the questionnaire, "When tape recording, what language did you mainly use for inner speech?" Based on their responses, we classified the 42 participants into four language groups: Chinese, English, Chinese mingled with English, and other languages. We compared participants' inaccuracy rates, obtained by dividing the number of errors by the overall number of lexical collocations they produced individually, among the language groups.

Our preliminary analysis discovered that the 42 participants produced a total of 2,491 lexical collocations, and each participant created approximately 29 lexical collocations per minute. Regarding learner errors, we found 263 incorrect collocations among the 2,491 lexical collocations, resulting in an inaccuracy rate of 10.56. To report the effect of language for thinking on the production of lexical collocations in speech, Table 5-1 records the fact that 5 students stated that their type of language for thinking was for the most part Chinese.

Table 5-1　Type of Language for Thinking and Inaccuracy Rates of Lexical Collocations

Group	N	M (%)	SD (%)	F	Comments
Chinese (CH)	5	15.17	5.48	4.07*	CH>CE*
English (EN)	17	12.40	6.72		EN>CE*
Chinese mingled with English (CE)	20	8.44	4.32		
Others	0				

Note: Mean shows the average inaccuracy rate of collocations in each group.

　　*$p<0.05$

As Table 5-1 shows, 17 mainly used English for thinking, 20 primarily thought in Chinese mingled with English, and none thought in other languages. We calculated the inaccuracy rate of oral lexical collocations in each language group by dividing the total number of lexical collocational errors by the total number of lexical collocations produced. Descriptive statistics demonstrated that those who mainly thought in their native language (Mandarin Chinese) produced the highest inaccuracy rate of lexical collocations (M=15.17), followed by those who primarily thought in English (M=12.40) and those using a combination

(M=8.44). Results of a one-way analysis of variance (ANOVA) further displayed that the difference among these three groups reached a significant level, $F(2, 39)=4.07$, $p<0.05$. This result supports the notion that EFL learners' type of language for thinking appreciably influences their oral production of lexical collocations.

To probe intergroup differences, we adopted the Fisher Least Significant Difference (LSD) post hoc test, which aims at discerning whether the comparison between groups reaches the significance level. The LSD test showed that the Chinese-mingled-with-English group had a markedly lower inaccuracy rate than the Chinese or English groups, while the difference between the Chinese and English groups was not significant. Thinking in both Chinese and English was more beneficial and effective to the EFL learners' oral production of lexical collocations.

Oral Elicitation Tasks and Lexical Collocational Errors

We measured the relationship between oral task and lexical collocation by comparing inaccuracy rates of lexical collocation under three speech conditions. The number of lexical collocations and errors and the inaccuracy rates in each task are shown respectively in Table 5-2.

Table 5-2　Differences Among Three Oral Elicitation Tasks in Inaccuracy Rates

Task Type	# of Collocations	# of Errors	%	M	SD	F
Picture description	786	82	10.43	10.23	8.80	0.58
Comic strip	742	72	9.70	10.23	8.42	
Prepared speech	963	109	11.32	11.86	8.82	

Note: % means the inaccuracy rate of lexical collocations in each task.

To ascertain if the task effect was statistically significant, we compared the 42 participants' data among the three speech conditions. The study found that they performed worst in prepared speech, and inaccuracy in this task was greater than in other tasks. We further employed a repeated-measures ANOVA to test differences across the three tasks. Table 5-2 plots the difference among the three oral elicitation tasks: It did not reach the significance level, F(2, 82)=0.58, $p>0.05$. This result indicates that the selection of oral elicitation tasks did not starkly influence the inaccuracy rate of lexical collocations.

Discussion

Types of Language for Thinking and Lexical Collocational Errors

The first research question investigated how learners' choice of language for thinking influences lexical collocation production. Statistically significant results revealed that learners primarily using Chinese mingled with English in thinking had the lowest inaccuracy rate, supporting the assumption that the type of language for thinking directly impacts oral lexical collocation. De Guerrero (1994) pointed out the major function of inner speech for metacognition. In general, speakers use their inner speech to plan, guide, and evaluate their own action. Inner speech in a way is the vehicle to help speakers form, develop, and voice their verbal thoughts. It facilitates SLA through the use of one's first language (L1) and the target language. Findings confirmed that learners can benefit while thinking in both the L1 and the target language, thus demonstrating inner speech as having cognitive and metacognitive support in speech production, especially in terms of oral lexical collocations. By contrast, if a learner primarily resorts to his or her L1, then oral production in English will depend on direct translation, causing a great deal of L1 interference at all linguistic levels. This finding accords with Goh's (2002) assumption that translation as a cognitive tactic slows down cognitive processing and distracts learners from some helpful linguistic clues. In the same vein, if English was used as the primary medium for thinking, then learners' nonnative, undeveloped English competence might also greatly hinder clear expression. In addition, as Brown (2001) stated, thinking in the target language may avoid the occurrence of some transfer errors from one's L1. Corresponding to Brown, this study argued that an optimal degree of inner speech in English can help speakers minimize lexical collocational errors in speech.

This study indicated an interesting finding: Thinking mainly in English was not beneficial for oral production of lexical collocations, even when learners were at the advanced level of proficiency. Although it was unexpected, the finding that those in the Chinese-mingled-with-English group performed best may have also provided a pedagogical suggestion that training EFL learners to think in English moderately can be helpful. To encourage thinking in English, educators can extend some of the metacognitive training activities proposed in Oxford (1990) to train learners' effective use of inner language. For instance, in a speaking task, while learners particularly at elementary and intermediate levels may often resort to their native language for thinking, instructors can encourage them to link the task with what they already know, such as familiar events and English phrases and sentences. On the one hand, talking about familiar events (e.g., things that the learner has experience with narrating in English) and using familiar English expressions require less processing time for translation. On the other hand, learners using language patterns they already know may present greater linguistic accuracy as well. With both advantages given, learners may resort less to direct translation from Chinese and engage a bit more in English. They may further reduce mistakes in oral production, like lexical collocational errors. Another crucial implication that may be drawn from our finding on the effect of language for thinking is that metacognitive skill training should be incorporated into ESL/EFL classrooms. Metacognitive skill refers to the "ability to think about thinking...[which] involves being aware of mental processes, monitoring them and controlling them" (Field, 2004, p.178). It is concerned with "knowing about learning and controlling learning through planning, monitoring, and evaluating the learning activity" (O'Malley, Chamot, & Küpper, 1989, p.422). Deeming metacognition an "executive" vehicle, Purpura (1997) also proposed that metacognitive strategies "involve planning for learning, thinking about the learning process as it is taking place, monitoring of one's production or comprehension, and evaluative learning after an activity is completed" (cited in Brown, 2000, p. 124). Metacognitive processes therefore help speakers plan, form, monitor, and evaluate their unshaped or shaped language internally. We argue for the importance of manipulating metacognitive activities in EFL classroom settings. For instance, based on the supportive role of language for thinking, instructors can employ task-based activities that coax learners into using L1 and target language support for inner speech. We believe that learners controlling their metacognitive skills will more effectively guide their own speech performance.

Oral Elicitation Tasks and Lexical Collocational Errors

The second research question asked whether the nature of oral elicitation task has any impact on how accurately EFL learners produce lexical collocations in speech. Results revealed a higher inaccuracy rate in prepared speeches than in picture-cued tasks. Still, no significant task effect of prepared speeches and picture-cued tasks on collocational accuracy emerged. This finding militates against general conclusions drawn by Nakahama et al. (2001) and Young and Milanovic (1992) that task selection influenced quality of talk. The latter examined the oral discourse structure of EFL learners and found task selection (e.g., task types) influencing quality and quantity, strongly arguing that task has the "strongest effect of any of the contextual variables considered" (p. 415). Yet task effect in this study did not confirm their research. We attribute this disagreement to the small number of participants: Only 42 subjects' data were collected and compared across three elicitation tasks. If more participants could be recruited, statistical difference among tasks might be more striking. While the statistical difference across three tasks was insignificant, the picture description task and comic strip storytelling undeniably yielded lower inaccuracy rates of lexical collocations, which could be ascribed to linguistic support of pictorial cues. Learners described what they saw, impelling them to process lower-level knowledge like lexicon and spend more cognitive capacity forming linguistic structures. In non-pictorial-supported prepared speech, we had supplied them with only a string of words as the question (word cues) to process both thoughts and language at the same time. This could easily exceed the maximum cognitive processing load they could handle. When facing this dilemma, our participants seemingly focused on ideational structures. They possessed less capacity to work out linguistic structures, which resulted in more collocational errors in prepared speech. To sum up, although task effect was not significant, comparing the inaccuracy rates in the three tasks indicates that processing demands of oral elicitation task may influence the quality of talk, including collocational accuracy.

(Adapted from Hung-ChunWang & Su-Chin Shih. 2011. The Role of Language for Thinking and Task Selection in EFL Learners' Oral Collocational Production. *Foreign Language Annals*, 4(2), 399–415.)

> Tasks

❶ **Read the first paragraph in the results section of the sample reading. Identify the information elements in each sentence of the paragraph.**

Sentences	Information Elements
1	
2	

(Continued)

Sentences	Information Elements
3	
4	

❷ Some verbs can be used to locate the results of the research, such as "show" and "indicate". Read the second and third paragraphs in the results section and find the verbs that the authors used to show the results.

1) _____

2) _____

3) _____

4) _____

5) _____

6) _____

❸ Read the discussion section and match the information elements in the box with the sentences taken from this section. Put the correct letter before the corresponding sentence.

a   possible explanations for the finding(s)

b. the new finding(s) which is/are different from previous studies

c. a reference to the main purpose/research questions of the study

d. a review of the most relevant/important finding(s)

e. a comparison between expected results and other studies

f. a summary of the finding(s)

_____ 1) The first research question investigated how learners' choice of language for thinking influences lexical collocation production.

_____ 2) Statistically significant results revealed that learners primarily using Chinese mingled with English in thinking had the lowest inaccuracy rate, supporting the assumption that the type of language for thinking directly impacts oral lexical collocation.

_____ 3) This finding accords with Goh's (2002) assumption that translation as a cognitive tactic slows down cognitive processing and distracts learners from some helpful linguistic clues.

_____ 4) While the statistical difference across three tasks was insignificant, the picture description task and comic strip storytelling undeniably yielded lower inaccuracy rates of lexical collocations, which could be ascribed to linguistic support of pictorial cues.

_____ 5) This study indicated an interesting finding: Thinking mainly in English was not beneficial for oral production of lexical collocations, even when learners were at the advanced level of proficiency.

_____ 6) To sum up, although task effect was not significant, comparing the inaccuracy rates in the three tasks indicates that processing demands of oral elicitation task may influence the quality of talk, including collocational accuracy.

III Language Focus

A. Comparison and Contrast

When you are writing the results section, you need to do much more than just give data. What you should always try to do is to convey more information with the data. Comparing and contrasting is a common way to deal with the data. Generally, the purpose of comparison is to show similarities while contrast is used to show differences. Through making comparison or contrast between two or more things, the readers can understand them better.

Here are some commonly used words and expressions to show comparison or contrast.

Words and Expressions Showing Comparison	Words and Expressions Showing Contrast
like; too; similar to; similarly; both; likewise; as well as; also; in the same way; have...in common; the same as	although; yet; whereas; however; but; while; instead; unlike; unless; be different from; the reverse; differ; contrary to; conversely; even though; on the contrary; on the other hand

Comparison and contrast is often used in graph description. Here are some points for you to pay special attention to.

First, not all the information has to be compared or contrasted with each other. It is common to introduce the most significant or important information and compare or contrast it. If necessary, you must make some calculations before comparing or contrasting the data.

Second, when you compare or contrast information in the graphs, it is not necessary to lay equal emphasis on every change. Just lay stress on those dramatic changes or on those that are of special interest to you, or those that you want your readers to pay more attention to and ignore the less important parts.

Third, the comparison or contrast should be supported by concrete and relevant facts or data.

> **Tasks**

❶ **The following sentences are taken from the sample reading. Underline the expressions that are applied to show comparison or contrast.**

1) By contrast, if a learner primarily resorts to his or her L1, then oral production in English will depend on direct translation, causing a great deal of L1 interference at all linguistic levels.

2) This finding accords with Goh's (2002) assumption that translation as a cognitive tactic slows down cognitive processing and distracts learners from some helpful linguistic clues.

3) Results revealed a higher inaccuracy rate in prepared speech than in picture-cued tasks.

❷ The following is a result from a market survey of personal computers. Report the result from a university student's perspective. First, describe students' needs in personal computers. Then compare and contrast the three types of personal computers. Finally, conclude by stating which computer seems to be the most suitable for the students' needs you have described.

A Market Survey of Personal Computers

Types	Price (yuan)	Hard Disk	Screen Size (inch)
PC 1	2,850	500 GB	14
PC 2	6,600	1,000 GB	15.6
PC 3	3,920	1,000 GB	14

Note: PC= personal computer.

_____

_____

_____

_____

_____

_____

_____

_____

_____

B. Cause and Effect

A cause-and-effect relationship is a relationship in which one event (the cause) makes another event happen (the effect). In the results and discussion section, the authors need to provide the reasons/causes for the results/effects, so the cause-effect relationships are commonly shown here.

In English, we have many approaches to show the cause-effect relationship. For example:

- The death rate from cancer is increasing *because* people are smoking more.

- The weather was cold. *Therefore,* Sally put on her coat.

- Many hair problems *result from* what you eat.

- The sports meeting was postponed *because of/due to* the rain.

❭ Tasks

❶ The following sentences are taken from the sample reading. Underline the expressions that are applied to show cause or effect.

1) Regarding learner errors, we found 263 incorrect collocations among the 2,491 lexical collocations, resulting in an inaccuracy rate of 10.56.

2) They possessed less capacity to work out linguistic structures, which resulted in more collocational errors in prepared speech.

❷ Complete the following paragraph by filling in causal words.

Recurring headaches can have initiated disruptive effects in a person's life. Firstly, in many cases, these headaches make a person nauseous to the point that he or she must go to bed. Furthermore, sleep is often interrupted 1)_____the pain. Disrupted sleep worsens the physical and emotional state of the sufferer. For those who try to maintain a normal lifestyle, drugs are often relied on to get through the day. Such drugs, of course, can 2)_____other negative effects. Drugs can inhibit productivity on a job, perhaps even 3)_____regular absences. Not only is work affected, but the seemingly unpredictable occurrence of these headaches 4)_____disruption in family life. The interruption to a person's family life is enormous: cancelling plans in the last minute and straining relationships with friends and family. It is no wonder that many of these people feel discouraged and even depressed 5)_____the cycle of misery reoccurring headaches cause.

A. Describing the Graphic Information

The results section clearly presents the results of your study. The results are usually reported both in the graphs and in the texts. You need to make some preparations before you report the results. First, prepare the graphs as soon as all the data are analyzed and arrange them in the sequence that best presents your results in a logical way. Then, prepare useful expressions and sentence patterns of graphic description. As the results section is a text-based section, the description of graphs is of great importance in paper writing. Good descriptions can help the readers understand your research better while using a single sentence pattern to describe the statistical and graphic information in a research paper will make your readers feel too bored and lose interest in reading on. Therefore, you need to pay more attention to the language use when describing the statistical and graphic information.

Here we will introduce some useful words, phrases, and sentence patterns which can be used in different situations of graphic description.

Situations	Expressions
When introducing the graphic information and making a general statement	The chart shows the percentage of... The vertical axis shows... The horizontal axis compares...
When referring to a graph	As can be seen/It can be seen from the graph... As shown in Graph 3, ... From the graph above, it may/can be seen/concluded/ shown/estimated/calculated/inferred that... The graph shows/presents/provides that... The graph below/The pie chart above shows/ illustrates... According to Table 1, ...

(Continued)

Situations	Expressions
When describing a graph	There was a minimal/slight/slow/gradual/steady rise. There was a rapid increase. There was a(n) marked/large/dramatic/steep/sharp/abrupt decrease/decline/reduction/fall/drop. There was a sudden fluctuation.
When describing a curve or a trend	a gradual/slight increase; a sharp/steep rise; the peak; a rapid/abrupt fall; a slight dip; no change; It shows an upward trend. It shows a downward trend.
When making a conclusion	to sum up in conclusion; It appears that...

The description of graphs is of great importance in paper writing because it can help the readers understand your research better. Then how do you describe a graph? Here are the major steps for you to follow:

- **Step 1:** Introduce the graphic information briefly and indicate the main trend. Normally it includes the place, the time, the content, and the purpose of the graph.

- **Step 2:** Describe the relevant and the most important data and make some comparisons if necessary. Words and expressions for describing a curve or a trend are very useful in presenting graphic information.

- **Step 3:** Summarize the data or trends.

If you need to highlight significant data in a table or chart, you may use some adjectives such as "apparent" "clear" "interesting" "obvious" "revealing" and "significant" to make your viewpoint known and meanwhile attract readers' attention. The following sentence patterns are useful when you report significant results or findings.

- It is *apparent* from Table 2 that...

- Table 5 is quite *revealing* in several ways.

- From Chart 5 we can see that Experiment 2 resulted in the *lowest* value of...

- What is *interesting* in this data is that...

- In Figure 10, there is a *clear* trend of decreasing...

- As Table 2.1 shows, there was a *great* difference between the experimental group and the control group.

- As shown in Table 6.3, chunk frequency also has a *significant* correlation with the indices of oral proficiency.

- There was no *obvious* difference between Method 1 and Method 2.

> Tasks

❶ The following line graph shows an upward trend in the growth rate of Ford car production in 2018. Analyze the line graph and fulfill the following tasks.

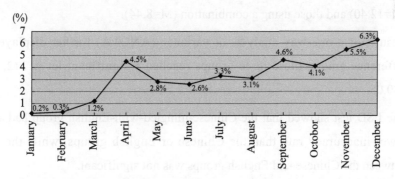

1) Mark the following positions in the graph.

   a. The bottom of the line;

   b. The peak of the line;

   c. The fluctuating part.

2) Describe the growth rate of Ford car production in the following months respectively. Try to use the phrases or sentence patterns of graphic description that you learned in this unit.

   a. In January: _____

   _____

   b. From March to April: _____

   _____

    c. From May to September: _____

_____

    d. From October to December: _____

_____

3) What does the overall line graph reveal in the growth rate of Ford car production in 2018?

_____

❷ **The following sentences are taken from the sample reading. Underline the expressions that are applied to highlight the significant data of the research.**

1) Descriptive statistics demonstrated that those who mainly thought in their native language (Mandarin Chinese) produced the highest inaccuracy rate of lexical collocations (M=15.17), followed by those who primarily thought in English (M=12.40) and those using a combination (M=8.44).

2) Results of a one-way analysis of variance (ANOVA) further displayed that the difference among these three groups reached a significant level, $F(2, 39)=4.07$, $p<0.05$.

3) The LSD test showed that the Chinese-mingled-with-English group had a markedly lower inaccuracy rate than the Chinese or English groups, while the difference between the Chinese and English groups was not significant.

4) Statistically significant results revealed that learners primarily using Chinese mingled with English in thinking had the lowest inaccuracy rate, supporting the assumption that type of language for thinking directly impacts oral lexical collocation.

5) By contrast, if a learner primarily resorts to his or her L1, then oral production in English will depend on direct translation, causing a great deal of L1 interference at all linguistic levels.

B. Strengthening or Weakening a Claim

The discussion section of a research paper focuses on making claims and then adding support for those claims. What are claims? Claims are statements about ideas and data from you and other people. Here is an example of a basic claim:

- An increase in smoking among teenagers caused long-term health problems.

When the proof of your idea or data is clear, you should strengthen your claim. When the evidence is less certain, you should limit or weaken your claim. Below are some examples of strengthening or weakening the claim above.

You can add some expressions before or after some parts of the sentence to strengthen the claim. For example:

- increase: a sharp increase

- caused: undeniably caused; clearly caused; undoubtedly caused;

- health problems: long-term health problems; widespread long-term health problems

You can also add expressions to the beginning of the sentence. For example:

- It is clear that an increase...

Here are the possible words for strengthening a claim.

Nouns	certainty; evidence
Verbs	prove; establish; confirm; conclude; determine
Adjectives	key; central; crucial; basic; fundamental; major; principal; essential; significant
Adverbs	very; quite; clearly; obviously; undoubtedly; certainly; indeed; inevitably; invariably; always; literally

Likewise, you can add some expressions before or after some parts of the sentence to weaken the claim. For example:

- increase: a probable increase
- caused: may have caused; seemed to have caused; was one cause of...

Again, you can add expressions to the beginning of the sentence. For example:

- We have reason to believe that an increase...
- It is possible that an increase...

Here are the possible words for weakening a claim.

Verbs	appear; argue; doubt; estimate; seen (as); seem; speculate; suggest
Adverbs	largely; likely; mainly; maybe; perhaps; possibly; probably; rather; relatively; seemingly; somewhat; sometimes

> **Tasks**

❶ **The following sentences are taken from the discussion section of a research paper. Underline the expressions that are applied to strengthen or weaken claims. Then mark them in the brackets at the end of each sentence. The first one is given as an example.**

1) We observed borderline <u>statistically significant</u> elevated risks for... (strengthening a claim)

2) We observed a stronger positive association for... (   )

3) It is possible that the referent group had a smaller-than-expected cancer incidence by chance. (   )

4) We observed a suggestion of an elevated risk for advanced prostate cancer with both meat types. (   )

5) In contrast to our findings, childhood leukemia has been positively associated with intake of processed meats in a case-control study. (   )

6) Associations between saturated fat and cancer are likely to be related to energy balance in general, whereas iron is thought to contribute to carcinogenesis specifically by generating free radicals and inducing oxidative stress. (   )

7) This could explain some of the inconsistencies in the literature as most previous studies have not specifically addressed advanced prostate cancer. (   )

8) It lends strong support to... (   )

9) We found a positive association between red meat intake specifically and cancers of the esophagus and liver... (   )

❷ The following sentences are taken from the sample reading. Write down the reasons why the authors weakened the claims.

1) Another crucial implication that may be drawn from our finding on the effect of language for thinking is that metacognitive skill training should be incorporated into ESL/EFL classrooms.

2) When facing this dilemma, our participants seemingly focused on ideational structures.

_____

_____

_____

_____

C. Outlining the Results and Discussion Section

Outlining the results and discussion section is very important because there is much work to do with the results and data collected. Meanwhile, you need to connect this section with the previous sections to ensure that the results collected are closely related to your research purpose and research questions.

When you outline the results and discussion section, there are usually four major moves to follow.

Move 1: Prepare the information.

Before writing the results and discussion section of your research paper, you need to make everything ready and ask yourself some questions concerning the preparation for writing this section. The following steps may be helpful for your preparation.

- **Step 1:** Review your results and check whether they have answered all the research questions. Do your results provide answers for your testable hypotheses?

- **Step 2:** Organize your results in a logical manner, Do you organize the results according to the priority or the importance of research questions? Do you organize the results according to the different research methods applied in your research?

- **Step 3:** Read the literature review section again. Do your findings agree with what others have shown? If not, do they suggest an alternative explanation or perhaps an unforeseen design flaw in your experiment (or theirs)?

- **Step 4:** Read the introduction section again. Regarding your conclusion, what is your new understanding of the problem you investigated and outlined in the introduction section? If warranted, what would be the next step in your study?

This move functions as a reminder and a connector between the method section and the results section, as it provides relevant information for the presentation of the results. It provides a review of issues mentioned in the methodology section, the location of the tables or the graphs where the results are displayed, and a general preview of the section. However, it is not obligatory because not all journal papers include this move in the results section.

Move 2: Report the results.

Move 2 is the core element. It is the move in which the results of a study are presented, normally with relevant evidence such as statistics and examples. In this move, you need to select the results which are closely related to your research purpose and research questions. After that, you need to locate where the results are and clearly describe the findings of the study both in diagrams and in the text.

You may refer to the introduction of describing the graphic information in this unit to get the skills of graphic description.

Move 3: Comment on the results.

This move serves the purpose of establishing the meaning and significance of the research results in relation to the relevant field. It includes the information and the interpretations that go beyond the "objective" results. This can involve how the results can be interpreted in the context of the study, how the findings contribute to the field (often involving comparison with related literature), what underlying reasons may account for the results. Also, comments about the strength, limitations, or generalizability of the results may be added in the move.

Move 4: Summarize the results and the discussion.

In this move, the major results obtained may be summarized in order to help readers understand the research better. This move is optional in a journal paper due to the limited length while it is a must for a dissertation or thesis.

After you finish outlining this section, you may pay attention to the following aspects when writing:

- The structure of the results and discussion section and the sequence of the presentation of the results;
- The choice of the appropriate language style in the results and discussion section;
- The revision of the draft of your work.

You can present the results and discussion section of your research paper in class, and then revise it according to the comments and the suggestions from your teacher and classmates.

> **Tasks**

❶ **Work in groups and discuss what other preparations you can make for writing the results and discussion section of your research paper.**

❷ **Discuss the following questions with your classmates.**

1) Which do you think is the most important move when outlining the results and discussion section? Why?

2) What aspects should be paid attention to when you write the results and discussion section?

本章配套资源

UNIT 6
Research Conclusion

Warm-up

In research papers, the conclusion section is a most valuable part. All the material that you have collected means nothing to readers until you present the conclusion as a result of your research. Conclusion is usually a brief section of academic texts which normally serves the following functions. The first is to summarize and bring together the main areas covered in the writing, which might be called "looking back". The second is to analyze and evaluate your main points for readers. In addition, you have to point out the general implications and possible limitations of your research in the conclusion. Finally, your conclusion may also include making suggestions for improvement and speculating on future directions. It manifests the value of your research as well as your understanding of the material that you have presented. It should be a strong recapitulation of your major points. But never add a new idea just because you have thought of it at the end!

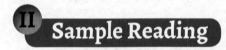

Sample Reading

Parental Phenol Exposure and Spontaneous Abortion in Chinese Population Residing in the Lower Reach of Yangtze River

Conclusion

By examining the relationships between a wide range of phenols widely used and spontaneous abortion, we found that paternal PCP exposure and maternal exposure to 4-n-OP and AP(s) were positively associated with spontaneous abortion. This study provided the first human data on the associations between both parental exposure to environmental phenols and spontaneous abortion. Although the adverse effect of maternal OP exposure on spontaneous abortion has not been well studied in humans, post-implantation embryonic loss caused by OP exposure during early pregnancy has been identified in rats. Some possible causes contribute to the relationships we observed between OP and AP(s) exposure and risk of spontaneous abortion. Besides, OP and NP possess higher endocrine-disruption potency and can easily pass through the placenta. Therefore, it may cause spontaneous abortion by affecting steroid receptors responsible for fetal programming on growth and immune function. Moreover, OP and NP may also cause spontaneous abortion by adversely affecting the reproduction and embryonic developmental stages through mitotic anomalies. In this study, a strong correlation between AP(s) (exposure to at least one of the two APs including 4-n-OP and 4-n-NP) and spontaneous abortion was observed, suggesting no maternal AP exposure may significantly decrease the risk of spontaneous abortion. In addition, experiments demonstrated that PCP could cause chromosome aberrations, DNA damage, and mutations. Thus, it is biologically plausible that paternal PCP exposure may increase the risk of spontaneous abortion by causing chromosome aberrations or impairing sperm quality.

The strengths of this study are the use of internal exposure estimation about various environmental phenols and simultaneous determination of both maternal and paternal exposure to phenols. The major limitations of our study are the relatively small sample size and its cross-sectional design which restricts the ability to make causal conclusion. Because biological samples (urine) of study population were required, the hospital-based design was selected. In fact, hospital controls may not be completely representative of the study population because it is not a random sample from all the target population. To address this limitation, we have restricted the study population to registered Nanjing residents, and the recruited controls were from the same hospital from which the cases originated. In order to further control the effect of potentially confounding factors, we included the variables which were statistically different between the case and control individuals as adjusted variables including paternal smoking, maternal BMI, and alcohol use. When compared with a random sample from all the target population, a hospital-based control might have underestimated the actual effects to some unknown extent. We recommend that further investigation is needed to elucidate the mechanisms linking paternal exposure to PCP, maternal exposure to 4-n-OP and AP(s) with spontaneous abortion.

(Adapted from Chen, X. J. et al. 2013. Parental Phenol Exposure and Spontaneous Abortion in Chinese Population Residing in the Lower Reach of Yangtze River. *Chemosphere,* 93: 217–222.)

> **Tasks**

❶ Read the conclusion section of the sample reading to identify the information elements in the following table. Then discuss their functions.

Information Elements	Relevant Details
Summary of the major findings	
Discussion of the major findings	
Implication of the research	
Limitations of the research	
Recommendation for further research	

❷ What verb tenses are mainly used in this conclusion section? Which one is predominant in this section, the active voice or the passive voice? Why?

_____

_____

_____

III Language Focus

A. Summarizing

There are three ways to include source material in academic writing: summarizing, paraphrasing, and quoting. Each of these strategies capitalizes on different types of information that can be useful. To summarize is to bring out in your own words a shortened version of written or spoken material, stating the main points and leaving out anything that is not essential. Summarizing is more than retelling; it involves analyzing information, distinguishing important elements from unimportant ones and transforming large chunks of information into a few short cohesive sentences. Look at the following example:

- **Original:** This effort to communicate—first through spoken messages, then through pictographs, then through the written word, and finally through printed words—demonstrates people's innate desire to share information with one another. Storability, portability, and accessibility of information are essential to today's concept of mass communication. (Shirley Biagi. *Media Impact: An Introduction to Mass Media*, 2nd edition, p. 24)

- **Summary:** In *Media Impact,* Shirley Biagi explains that people have always had an inherent need to communicate. The ability to store, carry, and have access to information is necessary in modern mass communication.

There are several techniques to be used when summarizing a text and they all stress full understanding of a text and require readers to spot the main points in it. Here are some useful tips for summarizing:

- Start by reading a short text and highlight the main points as you read;
- Read the text again and make notes of the main points, leaving out examples, evidence, etc;
- Restate or repeat the main points by using different words and phrases;
- Do not add your own ideas, opinions, or judgment of the arguments;
- Make it shorter than the original version.

Tasks

❶ **Read the following paragraph and write a summary of it.**

I come from India, but I have lived in Canada for several years now. I am surprised at how Canadian society respects the rights of women, both at work and at home. Personally I believe women in Canada are better off than women in India. However, some of my female friends in Canada miss the good old days when women were treated in a different way. You see, in the past, gentlemen followed different rules of behavior. They would open the doors for ladies, pull out chairs for ladies to sit down, stand up when a lady left the table, and offer to pay the bill at restaurants. Now, however, most Canadians believe that men and women should be considered equal. For example, women now generally have to pay for their own meals.

_____

_____

_____

_____

_____

_____

_____

_____

❷ **Read the following original paragraph and different summaries of it. Then decide which is the acceptable one and why.**

Original: Most medical people despised the press, holding attitudes not totally unfamiliar today. Reporters tended to be suckers for every quack, half-quack, over-eager scientist, or naive country doctor who thought he had a serum to cure tuberculosis, a herbal remedy for cancer, or a new surgical procedure to rejuvenate the aged. When the newspapers were not wasting space on undeserving medical stories, they were over-playing legitimate news, getting their facts wrong, and generally making a nuisance of themselves interfering in the lives and practices of busy professionals. Doctors' deep suspicion of what they read in the newspapers and even in the less-carefully edited medical journals helps to explain some of the early skepticism about insulin in countries like Britain: Oh, the Americans are always curing everything; this week it's diabetes. Even in Canada and the United States it was some months before there was enough confirmation of the unlikely news from Toronto to convince wire services and the more skeptical doctors and editors that insulin was, indeed, the real thing. (Michael Bliss. *The Discovery of Insulin*. Toronto: McClelland & Stewart, 1982. Chapter 8, Section I, Paragraph 1, Page 190)

Summary 1: Most medical people hated the press, because reporters tended to believe every over-eager scientist or naive country doctor who thought he had a cure for something. Newspapers often over-played legitimate news, got their facts wrong, and interfered in the lives and practices of busy professionals. Doctors became deeply suspicious of what they read in the newspapers and less-carefully edited medical journals, therefore were skeptical about insulin in countries like Britain because it seemed the Americans were always curing everything.

Summary 2: Most medical people hated the press, because reporters tended to believe every "over-eager scientist or naive country doctor" (p. 190) who thought he had a cure for something. Newspapers often over-played legitimate news, got their facts wrong, and interfered "in the lives and practices of busy professionals" (p. 190). Doctors became deeply suspicious of what they read in the newspapers and less carefully edited medical journals, therefore were skeptical about insulin in countries like Britain because it seemed the Americans were "always curing everything" (p. 190).

Summary 3: Insulin as a treatment for diabetes was not widely accepted as "the real thing" (p. 190) by the medical profession for many months after "the unlikely news from Toronto" (p. 190). Doctors had become skeptical about the legitimacy of medical discoveries as reported both by newspapers, which tended to waste space on "undeserving medical stories" (p. 190), and by some less professional medical journals.

Summary 4: Insulin as a treatment for diabetes was not widely accepted for many months because doctors had become skeptical about the legitimacy of medical discoveries as reported both by newspapers and by some less professional medical journals (p. 190).

B. Paraphrasing

The *Oxford English Dictionary* defines a paraphrase as "an expression in other words, usually fuller and clearer, of the sense of any passage or text; a free rendering or amplification of a passage....[Paraphrasing is] to express the meaning of (a word, phrase, passage) in other words, usually with the object of fuller and clearer exposition so as to bring out the sense" (XI: 204). To paraphrase means to completely reproduce the original meaning in your own words (but never include your own opinion). Look at the following example and a paraphrase about it:

- **Original:** Aggressiveness, present in many male teenagers, has often been characterized as having a biological base. However, social study theorists Bandura and Walters (1959) did a study which indicated that aggressiveness might be a product of environment factors and especially, social reinforcement. In this study, they found that aggressive boys had encouragement from their parents to be aggressive outside their home. Since their fathers experienced vicarious gratification from hearing about their son's aggressive behavior, this provided reinforcement for the boys. (Cong, 2009, p. 337)

- **Paraphrase:** Social scientists have often described aggressiveness, which is evident in many adolescent boys, as having a biological component. However, the research completed by social study theorists Bandura and Walters (1959) showed that aggressiveness might result from factors in the environment and, in particular, social reinforcement. It was found in the study that young males who were aggressive had been encouraged by their parents to be aggressive away from their home. Their fathers received indirect pleasure from learning of their son's aggressive behavior. Consequently, the boys' behavior was reinforced by their fathers' experience.

There are basically two ways of paraphrasing: by making word-level transformations (and maintaining the original syntax) or by considering its "deep structure" and making more significant changes. Note how the following two versions of paraphrase differ:

- **Original:** The temperature in many parts of the world is gradually rising.

- **Paraphrase 1:** The temperature in lots of places around the earth is slowly increasing.

- **Paraphrase 2:** Most parts of the world are getting hotter steadily.

The first version represents a word-level paraphrase and the second version is a deep-level transformation. It is usually believed that making word-level paraphrases is easier than deep-level transformations.

Here are some guidelines for paraphrasing:

- Use synonyms;

- Change word forms;

- Make necessary structural adjustments;

- Change between the affirmative and the negative;

- Include references to the original source.

 Task

Read the following paragraph and try to paraphrase it.

Starting in the 15th century, the reality and the idea of the family were to change: a slow and profound revolution, scarcely distinguished by either contemporary observers or later historians, and difficult to recognize. And yet the essential event is quite obvious: the extension of school education. We have seen how in the middle ages children's education was ensured by apprenticeship in adults, and that after the age of seven, children lived in families other than their own. Henceforth, on the contrary, education became increasingly a matter for the school. The school ceased to be confined to clerics and became the normal instrument of social initiation, of progress from childhood to manhood. (Aries, P. *Centuries of Childhood: A Social History of Family Life*. 1962)

IV Academic Writing Skills

A. Using Sentence Patterns

The italicized patterns and expressions in the following sentences are often used in writing conclusions. Try to use them in your own writing.

- This paper *has demonstrated* that the factors influencing the choice of both forms of direct address and terms of reference in a historical material *can be* measured by using present-day theoretical tools.

- *We have shown how* the quotient graph *can be used to reduce* model checking of TA to the untimed case, so that classical finite-state system verification techniques can be applied.

- *It was notable that* the non-feedback control group was more successful in finding and correcting word choice errors than any other error category.

- *We have examined the relationship between* students' self-assessments of their own writing problems, their preferences about error correction, *and* their prior knowledge about specific grammatical problems and the texts they produced.

- *In this paper, we proposed an idea* of role in the interaction of web services. On its basis, we can effectively check whether two or more web services are compatible in collaboration or not.

- *Experimental results* obtained by applying minim on a number of examples *have shown* that our approach is both general and practical. Reach ability analysis *is still preferable* for simple properties such as invariant or bounded response.

- *Much work needs to be done* to make these algorithms more efficient in practice.

- *By* examining primarily a controlled experimental feedback treatment, the present study *obviously has its limits.* But it *provides specific evidence* that can help teachers weigh some of their feedback options carefully. *Clearly, it also raises further questions for future investigations on this topic. It is to be hoped that* researchers will continue to pursue this research agenda for the benefit of teachers and students alike.

- *Several implications for future research work are suggested* by the findings, some of which are *in response to the limitations* of this study.

- *After all,* the bound for the grid size that we require is indeed very small. We hope that *there is room for some improvement.*

> **Task**

Complete the following conclusion by translating the Chinese in the brackets into English.

As a matter of fact, we only considered the compatibility and substitutability between two Web services. 1)_____ (当涉及更多网络 服务器时), it will be more complex and need more research. We also assume that messages communicate in a synchronous way. Reasoning on asynchronous communications raises very subtle problems and is 2)_____ (不幸的 是往往不可断定), which means that automated tools are submitted to severe restrictions. 3)_____ (另外一个研究方向是) that when two Web services are not compatible, it is natural to "do something" to correct the flaws in their interaction. Several authors have proposed some possibilities, 4)_____ (但这个问题仍 应进一步研究).

B. Restating the Research Objective

In the conclusion section, you need to restate your thesis statement. You should avoid repeating the thesis statement, otherwise your conclusion may sound boring or repetitive. Using a thesaurus is a good way to find new, interesting expressions. For example:

- This study set out to determine...

- The present study was designed to determine the effect of...

- In this investigation, the aim was to assess...

- The purpose of the current study was to determine...

- This project was undertaken to design...and evaluate...

- Returning to the hypothesis/question posed at the beginning of this study, it is now possible to state that...

Here are examples of research question and concluding statement:

- **Research question:** What is more important: competitive price, fuel economy, or high resale value when Chinese people buy cars?

- **Concluding statement:** The research set out to determine what factors contribute more to Chinese people's decision when purchasing cars: competitive price, fuel economy, or high resale value.

› Task

Write concluding statements based on the following research questions.

1) What in San Francisco attracts visitors more: the magnificent location, the theaters and art galleries, or the fine restaurants?

_____

_____

2) Do employees need to be trained for working in the Australian multicultural workplace? But managers also need to be trained.

_____

_____

3) What is the 2014 rate of juvenile delinquency in the U.S.?

_____

_____

4) Does education play a role in reducing juvenile delinquents' return to crime?

_____

_____

5) What marketing strategies does the Coca-Cola company currently apply?

_____

_____

6) Do children sent to daycare or preschool start kindergarten with more highly developed language skills?

_____

_____

7) How might the discovery of a genetic basis for obesity change the way in which we treat obese persons, both medically and socially?

_____

_____

C. Writing a Conclusion Section

The following are the points for attention in preparing the conclusion section:

- Be careful not to draw conclusions from data involving errors of observation;
- Do not use mathematical formulas without clear understanding of the derivations and all the assumptions involved;
- Avoid confusing facts with opinions of influences, not only in the investigation itself but also in preparing results for publication;
- Do not draw a conclusion from too few data, or too broad a conclusion that is based on extrapolated curves;
- Guard against failing to qualify a conclusion, in order to show the limits within which it applies, or the variation which is to be expected;
- When you indulge in a speculation, be sure to remind your reader that it remains a speculation.

Write a conclusion section based on the following discussion section of a paper.

The current research documented the impact of interventions designed to strengthen children's environmental identities through a case study approach involving a 5th grade class by examining strategies effective at enhancing children's relationship with the natural world. Data from written reflections and interviews with children and their teacher created specific positive impacts of the program on children's environmental identities and quantitative data supported these findings. This discussion focuses on identifying effective practices and addressing the ways these practices may have been particularly effective at impacting children's environmental identities. Finally, it considers the relationship between efforts to improve children's environmental identities and school science.

What intervention elements at the Center impacted children's environmental identities? The intervention included several strategies that seemed to be particularly significant in impacting children's environmental identities. These included locating the program in a natural outdoor setting, specifically addressing children's comfort in the natural world, providing time for shared reflections of feelings about nature, incorporating free-choice learning opportunities with simple activities, and fostering social interactions between children as well as between the children and their adult leaders, including their classroom teacher. It was critical that the intervention to strengthen children's environmental identities took place in the outdoors. By locating the program in the outdoors, children had opportunities for direct contact with the natural world, enabling them to see, feel, touch, smell, hear, and appreciate the life around them, which was important in helping them develop positive feelings about nature as well as foster their interest in the organisms they encountered. The shared experiences in the outdoors also served as an anchor for the teacher and children to connect science in their classroom with science in the natural world. The teacher, realizing the benefits of the outdoors for the children after witnessing their interactions there, expressed a desire to relocate some instruction outdoors and sought to grant funding to the Center after the conclusion of the study. This study suggests that a teacher's intent to situate science learning in the outdoors may be influenced by students' interaction with the natural world as well as coming to understand the importance they place on their relationship with nature.

How does an intervention designed to strengthen children's connection to nature impact children's interest in school science? If children saw their experience at the Center as distinct from their experience of school science, why did the intervention increase children's interest in school science? The increased interest in science was documented qualitatively and supported by increased mean science interest scores in the intervention group. However, it is important to acknowledge that the quantitatively measured increase in science interest in the intervention group was not statistically significant. It is possible that this measurement was limited by the small size of the intervention group, by the low number of visits to the Center, or by a ceiling effect.

The opportunity to explore science interest in the natural world, outside the science classroom but still as part of a school enterprise, may have expanded children's vision of what science at school could be. It helped the teacher make connections between the science they were learning in school and the natural world they experienced at the Center.

Based on the interviews with children, another possible explanation may account for observation of children's increased interest in science at school. The opportunities to be outside in nature, such as making observation, discussing feelings, and reflecting upon their experiences in the natural world in the social context of their class may have allowed children who had relatively silent feelings and interest in nature to share these with the class in a way that they were outwardly appreciated by the classroom teacher as well as by peers. Physically being outside in a learning situation changed how some children were viewed by both the teacher and other children partly because being outside freed many children from the stress they felt in science classroom. Discussions of feelings about the natural world changed how some children viewed themselves in relation to the natural world, especially their comfort levels and concern for the organisms at the Center. These changing feelings may have had the effect of strengthening children's environmental identities in the context of schooling, possibly improving their interest in school science.

Children's environmental identities are partly determined by their feelings about the natural world (Kals & Ittner, 2003). Researchers have suggested that neglecting the way children feel about the natural world may contribute to their alienation from school science (Cobern, 2000; Hammond, 2001). Though time constraints often limit science in elementary classrooms (Carrier et al, 2013), it can be specially important to address children's environmental identities at the elementary level, given the long-term goal of abating children's declining interest in science as they approach middle school.

Because of their interest in the natural world, it seems that children with strong environmental identities ought to be among our most interested science students. But sometimes they are not (Calabrese & Yang, 2000). The present research reveals several strategies used by environmental educators that hold potential for strengthening children's environmental identities as well as their interest in school science. The strategies include: relocating some instruction outdoors, particularly in natural settings; incorporating free-choice learning opportunities into science instruction; allowing for time and opportunities for social interaction; addressing children's comfort levels in the natural world, and giving children a chance to discuss and reflect upon their feelings about the natural world within the context of a school science experience. In this study, these strategies seemed to foster children's interest in science. Perhaps this is a step toward pursuing more scientific information over the course of their lifetime.

本章配套资源

UNIT 7
Abstract & Documentation

 Learning Objectives

- To understand the elements and features of an abstract;

- To become aware of the use of verbs and tenses in an abstract;

- To learn how to provide keywords in an abstract;

- To understand reference styles;

- To write an abstract and create a reference list.

Warm-up

Before you learn the detailed steps to write an abstract, please think about the following questions:

- Where can you find an abstract in a thesis or dissertation?
- What is the purpose of writing an abstract?
- What are the basic elements for an academic abstract?
- What language problems may you have in abstract writing? (For example, the wording problem, the tense problem, the voice problem, etc.)

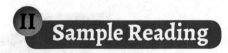

Sample Reading

The Self-Promotion of Academic Textbooks in the Preface Section: A Genre Analysis

Abstract: This paper presents a genre analysis of the preface section in academic textbooks, specifically twenty-two preface sections from the closely-related fields of linguistics and applied linguistics. With the adoption of the move structure analysis proposed by Swales (1990) and Bhatia (1993), four moves were identified to account for the different rhetorical purposes employed by writers of preface sections to create a niche and establish the importance of their textbooks. These moves comprise: establishing the needs of the readership, establishing their orientations like purpose and audiences, outlining of the scope of the chapters, and finally acknowledgments. This move structure reflects the textual strategies used by writers to achieve the rhetorical purposes of the preface sections. It is suggested that these findings could be incorporated into instructional literature for writers wishing to start book projects, and that they may also be helpful for English as a Foreign Language (EFL) teachers in selecting materials for their classrooms based on their external evaluation of academic textbooks.

Keywords: genre; preface; move; textual strategies; rhetorical purposes

(Adapted from Azar, A. S. 2012. The Self-Promotion of Academic Textbooks in the

Preface Section: A Genre Analysis. *Atlantis-Journal of the Spanish Association of Anglo-American Studies*, 30(2), 147–165.)

> **Tasks**

① What is the most suitable subject for the sample abstract?

    a. Computer Science

    b. Civil Engineering

    c. Applied Linguistics

    d. Chemistry Industry

② Answer the following questions based on the sample abstract.

    1) How was the study carried out?

    _____

    _____

    2) What did the study find?

    _____

    _____

    3) What is the use of the findings?

    _____

    _____

③ Match the information elements of an abstract in the box with the following sentences taken from the sample abstract.

a. background	b. objective	c. materials	d. approach
e. findings	f. conclusion	g. implication	h. limitation

_____ 1) This paper presents a genre analysis of the preface section in academic textbooks, specifically twenty-two preface sections from the closely-related fields of linguistics and applied linguistics.

_____ 2) With the adoption of the move structure analysis proposed by Swales (1990) and

Bhatia (1993), four moves were identified to account for the different rhetorical purposes employed by writers of preface sections to create a niche and establish the importance of their textbooks. These moves comprise: establishing the needs of the readership, establishing their orientations like purpose and audiences, outlining of the scope of the chapters, and finally acknowledgments.

_____ 3) This move structure reflects the textual strategies used by writers to achieve the rhetorical purposes of the preface sections.

_____ 4) It is suggested that these findings could be incorporated into instructional literature for writers wishing to start book projects, and that they may also be helpful for English as a Foreign Language (EFL) teachers in selecting materials for their classrooms based on their external evaluation of academic textbooks.

❹ **Look at the keywords in the sample abstract and decide what categories they belong to.**

Keywords	Categories
genre	
preface	
move	
textual strategies	
rhetorical purposes	

III Language Focus

Verbs, Sentence Patterns, and Verb Tenses

In writing an abstract, verbs, sentence patterns, and verb tenses should be considered carefully. The following two tables demonstrate some good points that you can refer to when writing an abstract. Table 7-1 presents verbs and sentence patterns and Table 7-2 is related to verb tenses.

Table 7-1　Verbs and Sentence Patterns in an Abstract

Information Elements	Verbs	Sentence Patterns
Background	originate, provide, summarize, review, ...	The theory comes/stems/emerges/originates from... The theory is obtained from...
Objective	develop, explain, address, aim, attempt, ...	This paper develops a theoretical framework to... This report/thesis/presentation...explains/outlines/ summaries/evaluates/surveys/develops/investigates/ discusses/focuses on...the results of...
Research focus(es)	present, discover, include, study, ...	The chief aim/main purpose/primary object/major objective/ principal goal of the study is to present... The main purpose of this essay is to discover...
Research process	examine, conduct, analyze, discuss, consider, investigate, ...	Firstly, ...was examined..., and then, the experiment on... was conducted. After...was analyzed, the results were discussed. Before the questionnaire was designed, ...must be considered.

(Continued)

Information Elements	Verbs	Sentence Patterns
Methods	observe, collect, estimate, calculate, measure, ...	The curative effect/sensitivity/function of certain drug/kit/organ was observed/detected/studied. The experiment was designed to collect the data on...
Research results	show, present, indicate, demonstrate, illustrate, imply, ...	It has been found/observed/proved/shown that... These experiments indicate/reveal/show/demonstrate that... The approach/method/framework promises to be... The results show/indicate/suggest that... It is shown/concluded/proposed that... This could imply that... These studies are of significance to... These results have direct application to...
Conclusion	summarize, introduce, conclude, ...	This article summarizes... The experiment has introduced... This causes/results in/leads to/brings about/gives rise to... The data leads us to a conclusion that... The data enables us to conclude that...

Table 7-2　Verb Tenses in an Abstract

Types of Information	Verb Tenses	Examples
Giving background details	The simple present tense	The industry <u>is</u> already well known for its efforts to improve the eco-efficiency of its processes.
Describing research activities	The simple past tense; the present perfect tense (sometimes the simple present tense according to the journal's requirements)	The study <u>focused</u> on two main areas. The framework for life cycle analysis <u>has been developed</u>.

(Continued)

Types of Information	Verb Tenses	Examples
Describing methods	The simple past tense (active or passive) (sometimes the simple present tense according to the journal's requirements)	We carried out a series of field tests. A large number of samples were tested for fracturing.
Reporting results	The simple past tense (sometimes the simple present tense according to the journal's requirements)	Results indicated that the problem is even more serious than previously predicted. The third model proved to be more durable than the other four.
Stating conclusions	The simple present tense	This indicates that there are, in fact, several factors contributing to the decrease. It appears that the incidence of human error cannot be eliminated at any stage. There might be a need for revising the list of criteria within the next 5–10 years.

> Tasks

❶ **Read the sample abstract and find out the verbs and the sentence patterns. An example has been given for you.**

Abstract: The electrical and piezo-resistive responses of recycled carbon fiber (RCF)-reinforced concrete are analyzed in this article. Two different PAN-based RCFs (monofilament RCF and fibrillated RCF sheets) incorporated into dry concrete mix were investigated. Piezo-resistivity was evaluated by simultaneously monitoring the variation in the applied DC voltage during both flexural and compressive tests. Although both plain and RCF-reinforced concrete samples showed piezo-resistive responses, the latter showed increased signal-to-noise ratio and thus behaved like self-sensing materials. The electrical behavior suggests a mixed control owing to both ionic and electronic conductivity, with the dominant one depending on the RCF content and RCF dispersion. This work enhances the possibility of generalizing the use of smart cementitious materials in the civil engineering industry.

Keywords: reinforced concrete; piezo-resistivity; electronic conductivity; smart cementitious materials

(Adapted from Segura, I., Faneca, G., et al. 2019. Self-Sensing Concrete Made from Recycled Carbon Fibers. *Smart Materials and Structures,* 28(10).)

Verbs	Sentence Patterns
analyze	... are analyzed...

❷ **Read the abstract above again and check the verb tenses in it.**

Information Elements	Verb Tenses	Examples
Background		
Methods		

(Continued)

Information Elements	Verb Tenses	Examples
Results		
Conclusion		
Significance		

IV Academic Writing Skills

A. Preparing for Writing an Abstract

Now that you have learned about the information elements, verb tenses, sentence patterns, and keywords for an abstract, it seems that you have made a good preparation for writing an abstract and it is high time that you should write one. However, there must be a concrete process when you write an abstract.

> Task

Rearrange the following statements to form a reasonable process of writing an abstract.

_____ 1) Identify the major results from the discussion or results section.

_____ 2) Check to see if it meets the guidelines of the targeted journal.

_____ 3) Identify the major objectives and conclusions.

_____ 4) Remove extra words and phrases.

_____ 5) Identify phrases with keywords in the method section.

_____ 6) Assemble the above information into a single paragraph in a right information order with appropriate verbs, tenses, and sentence patterns.

_____ 7) Give the abstract to a colleague (preferably one who is not familiar with your work) and ask him/her whether it makes sense.

_____ 8) Revise the paragraph so that the abstract conveys only the essential information.

B. Outlining an Abstract

When outlining an abstract, you should include five major information elements, namely background, research objective, methods, results, and conclusion.

> **Task**

The following paper is finished without an abstract and keywords. Read the paper and find the related statements to fill in the table that follows the paper.

Study on the Network-Based English Phonetics Teaching Mode
for English-Major Students

1. Introduction

With the development of Information Technology, the Internet is accessible to all, especially to the students. Based on the network, English teaching is changing greatly, which is not simply with textbooks, chalk and blackboard, but with multimedia, various apps and other digital tools. For English-major students, the network-based teaching mode is playing a more important role, especially for the teaching of English phonetics.

In terms of nature and function, language is a system of code combining sound and meaning with speech sound as the material shell, vocabulary as the building block, and grammar as the structure law. Teaching of English-major students inevitably involves the teaching of phonetics. The wide use of multimedia technology has changed the situation of "dumb English" teaching which stresses grammar more than pronunciation. With the traditional class teaching, students are passive to listen and the teachers are teaching orally in class. However, the limitation of teachers' inaccuracy of pronunciation leads to the students' errors in pronunciation. Moreover, the students have less time to be corrected in time. The positive effect of computer-aided technology, multimedia-aided teaching technology, and the artificial intelligence-aided teaching technique used in English teaching has been verified by relevant scholars, but a number of researchers are still reforming and applying the network-based English teaching mode. Under the use of Information Technology, the trend of reforming in English teaching mode is inevitable to happen. The creation of a new teaching mode is one of the ways to the reform of English teaching.

The network-based English phonetics-teaching mode for English-major students can help the students learn better in English pronunciation than those who learn in the traditional mode. Thus, the current researchers studied the steps of the network-based teaching mode, the effectiveness of the network-based teaching mode, and selected the English-major college students of 2017 in Anhui Institute of Information Technology as the subjects of the teaching experiment to show the significance of the model.

2. Network-based Teaching Mode

The teaching mode is the theme of education. The network-based teaching mode which focuses on net learning is a reform to the traditional teaching mode. With the advantages, it is possible to achieve more effectiveness in teaching.

2.1 Theoretical Basis of Network-Based Teaching Mode

Constructivism is the theory proposed by cognitive psychologist Piaget who believed that teaching should be centered on the students. Students are becoming the active participants of the class instead of passive indoctrinators of knowledge. Teachers need to change to counsel students, to help and instruct learning instead of teaching knowledge. For constructivism, in the process of learning, the students' learning resources have been enlarged beyond textbooks, and the relationship involved in the teaching has been changed from one-way indoctrination to multi-directional interaction, interdependence, inter-conversion, teacher-student interaction, student-student interaction, and human-computer interaction. Obviously, the network-based English phonetics teaching mode provides an environment conforming to the constructivism theory and taking students as the center.

...

3. Experiment Design and Data Analysis

With the development of the society and the rapid growth of international integration, higher education meets the challenges greatly. As college teachers, we need to improve to meet the requirements brought by the rapid development. We should not only use the traditional teaching mode, but also use the network-based teaching mode to teach the students. Thus, the assessment of the network-based teaching mode is used in Anhui Institute of Information Technology. The authors implement the experiment through questionnaire investigations and data analysis to show the hypothesis that the network-based teaching mode can benefit students better than the traditional teaching mode.

3.1 Experiment Subjects

The experiment uses the English-major college students of 2017 from Anhui Institute of Information Technology as subjects. The total number of the students is 78 who are placed in two classes. Table 1 is the information about background and learning time. Table 2 is the one-way analysis of variance (ANOVA) on the average entrance score.

Table 1   Basic Information Between the Experiment Class and the Control Class

	Size of Class	Average Entrance Score	Weekly Extracurricular Speaking and Reading Time
Experiment class	38	105.5	1.3
Control class	40	106.7	1.5
Total	78	106.1	1.4

From Table 1 we can see that the two classes are similar in some ways. The size of the class, the average entrance score (total of 150), and the weekly extracurricular speaking and reading time are similar to each other for the two classes.

Table 2   One-way Analysis of Variance (ANOVA) on the Average Entrance Score

	Sum of Squares	df	Mean Square	F	*P*-value
Between groups	26.844	1	26.844		
Within groups	9047.874	76	119.051	0.225	0.636
Total	9074.718	77			

To get the one-way ANOVA on the average entrance score, the statistical software (SPSS) is used. From Table 2, we can see that $F=0.225<1$, $p=0.636>0.05$, which shows that little obvious differences exist in the two classes. As for this, we can have the experiment continued and look forward to the result of significant differences.

3.2 Experiment Process

The learning requirements for the experiment class and the control class are different. For the experiment class, the students are assigned to preview the lessons on the net, including watching the videos of English pronunciation, seeing the film of English version and dubbing the cartoons and TV plays in English. After finishing the assignments, the students should send the dubbing to the teachers by QQ or e-mail. In the class, the teacher delivers the theory of English pronunciation, let the students practice the pronunciation, and correct the incorrect pronunciation of the students. The teacher can also use the net in the class through multimedia to let the students dub the native speakers by groups. Thus, the teacher is the tutor in the class to instruct the pronunciation of the students, and the students are the center to do the exercises and practice of the pronunciation. After class, the students are asked to review the lessons on the net and finish the tasks assigned by the teachers through e-mail or BBS. The following figures give the examples of the experiment class teaching based on the net. Figure 1 is the assignments checking. Figure 2 shows the new points in learning the lessons.

Figure 1 shows that the teacher can check the assignments of dubbing through multimedia by clicking the start button and the students can dub the short video. This use of video can stimulate the students' interests in learning English phonetics, and through dubbing and imitating the native speakers, the students can speak English more effectively. After checking the assignments, the teacher uses a short time to illustrate the rules in pronunciation of the new knowledge, which is shown in Figure 2.

Figure 1   Dubbing the Short Video

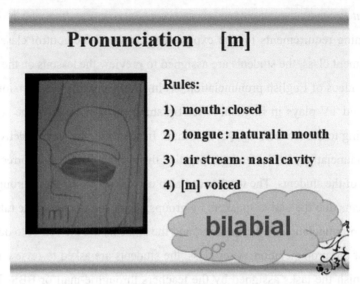

Figure 2   New Points of the Lesson

Figure 2 indicates that the consonant [m] is taught. In the PowerPoint, the teacher lists the rules in pronunciation and the classification of [m]. With the picture and the rules, the students can understand the pronunciation well and pronounce it correctly. After that the students will have more opportunities to practice the newly acquired knowledge.

On the other hand, the students in the control class have their lessons in the traditional classroom, with the teachers delivering lessons through textbooks, and blackboard and chalk. The assignments done by the students cannot be monitored by the teachers after class, but only in class. The teachers check the pronunciation homework in class and correct them within the short class period.

Meanwhile, questionnaires and investigation have been used to testify the attitude and learning autonomy of using the network-based teaching mode for the experiment class at both the beginning and the end of the semester in Anhui Institute of Information Technology. The investigations are aimed to measure ordinal variables to measure attitudes. At the end of the semester, the same examination of reading phonetic symbols, words, phrases, sentences, and paragraphs is conducted to testify whether the experiment class does better than the control class. Moreover, statistical software (SPSS) is used to collect and summarize data efficiently to get meaningful information and enhance the validity of the collected data.

3.3 Experiment Results

In order to find out the results of network-based teaching mode, the questionnaire is used. There are 6 questions. Questions 1 to 3 are used to ascertain the purpose, the average time, and the study scope of the students for using the net, which aims to get the information on students' learning autonomy. Questions 4 to 6 are used to ascertain the acceptance, the effectiveness, and the recommendation of net learning, which aims to get the information on students' attitude toward the network-based teaching mode. Thirty-eight questionnaire forms are distributed and collected, and all are valid. Table 3 shows the result of Questions 1 to 3. Table 4 presents the result of Questions 4 to 6.

Table 3　Results from the Questionnaire for the Information of Students' Learning Autonomy

Item	Purpose of Using Net (%)			Average Time Online per Week (%)			Scope of Study Online (%)		
	Study	Amusement	Others	Zero	5–8 hrs	> 8 hrs	English	Chinese	Others
Beginning	21.1	55.3	23.6	13.2	63.2	23.6	30.4	60.5	21.1
End	65.8	18.4	15.8	0.0	71.1	28.9	80.9	10.5	5.3

From Table 3 we can see that at the beginning of the semester, most of the students use net for amusement and only 21.1% of the students use it for study. However, at the end of the semester, most of the students use the net to learn, which accounts for 65.8%. Students using the net to study increase by 44.7%. As to the average time of the students at the beginning of the semester, 13.2% of the students do not use the net, but at the end of the semester, there is no one who does not use the net. This is the significant change of using the new mode on the part of the students. Of course, for the learning subject at the end of the semester, the students pay much more attention to English partly because they are English majors.

Table 4   Results from the Questionnaire for the Attitudes of Students' Net Learning

Item	Acceptance (%)			Effectiveness (%)			Recommendation (%)		
	Totally	Agree	Disagree	High	Med.	Low	Strongly	Willing	Unwilling
Beginning	15.8	73.7	10.5	13.2	57.9	28.9	7.9	47.4	44.7
End	26.3	71.1	2.6	26.3	65.8	7.9	23.6	63.2	13.2

Table 4 reveals the result of the students' attitudes toward the network-based teaching mode. At the beginning of the semester, only 15.8% of the students accept net learning and 10.5% of the students do not accept it. However, at the end of the semester, the total acceptance rate increases by 10.5% and the non-acceptance rate decreases by 7.9%. From the changes in percentage we can see that most of the students accept the new mode of net learning. As for the effectiveness of net learning, at the end of the semester, the percentage of the students who think that net learning has high effectiveness increases by 13.1%, whereas the percentage of the students who think that net learning has low effectiveness decreases by 21.0%. From the change, we can see that the students can benefit immensely from net learning, thus 86.8% of the students are willing or strongly willing to recommend the use of net learning. We still see that some of the students do not accept and are unwilling to recommend net learning to their friends. The authors ask about the reasons. From the investigation, the authors observe that they lack searching skills on the net, so that they waste their time in learning. Therefore, the authors believe that how to use net effectively is to be taught to the students.

Table 5   Scores of the Final Examination

Class	Number of Students	Highest Score	Lowest Score	Average Score
Experiment class	38	90	53	73.8
Control class	40	93	48	69.3
Total	78	93	48	71.5

After analyzing the students' attitude and the learning habits, the authors aim to find out whether the network-based teaching mode stimulates the students and whether the students' reading ability is improved. Thus, the same examination is to be taken by all the students. As is shown in Table 5, at the end of the semester, the scores of the experiment class and the control class are different. Although there is a student who gets the highest score 93 in the control class, the average score of the examination of the experiment class (73.8) is higher than that of the control class (69.3). It shows that network-based teaching mode can provide effectiveness in English phonetics learning for English majors.

Table 6　One-way Analysis of Variance (ANOVA) on the Average Final Score

Class	Sum of Squares	df	Mean Square	F	*P*-value
Between groups	392.771	1	392.771		
Within groups	7458.716	76	98.141	4.002	0.049
Total	7851.487	77			

To see whether there is significant difference between the control class and the experiment class, the ANOVA on the average final score is analyzed. From Table 6, we can see that F=4.002>1, and p=0.049<0.05, which shows that obvious differences exist in the two classes. The network-based English phonetics teaching mode can lead to effective study.

4. Conclusion

Through the experiment and data analysis, we find that the network-based teaching mode can benefit students better than the traditional teaching mode. It helps the English majors to have access to more learning resources, to speak English in a more effective manner, and to develop the habit of autonomous learning. Meanwhile it helps the teacher conduct a reform in English phonetics teaching and devote more time to research.

...

(Adapted from Wang, Y. W. & Zhou, H. S. 2019. Study on the Network-Based English Phonetics Teaching Mode for English-Major Students. *International Journal of Emerging Technologies in Learning,* 14(5): 165–175.)

Information Elements	**Examples**
Background	
Research objective (aim)	
Methods (procedure, methodology)	
Results (findings, product)	
Conclusion (implication)	

C. Drafting an Abstract Together with Keywords

Now that we have learned how to prepare for drafting an abstract and how to find out the five basic information elements for an abstract, it's time for us to draft an abstract with keywords.

❯ Task

Draft an abstract together with keywords for the paper based on the table above.

_____

_____

_____

_____

_____

_____

D. Making a Reference List

All of the sources you refer to in the main body of your paper need to be listed at the end on a reference list. On this list, you need to list those sources from which you have either quoted or paraphrased.

A reference includes at least the following three functions:

- First, it is used to avoid plagiarism;
- Second, it tells editors and readers what sources have been cited in the paper;
- Third, it can help readers to refer to the materials when they write papers.

And a good reference should adhere to the following three rules:

- First, it must be authoritative. Choosing an authoritative expert and an authoritative journal in a related field to refer to is quite safe and preferable when citing others' work.

- Second, it should be up-to-date. Except old but typical books or articles, your references should be of the latest study to convince your readers.

- Third, you can use two or three articles in the journal that you want to submit to as your references, which can help to enhance your target journal's influence.

There are at least two different types of references. The Institute of Electrical and Electronics Engineers (IEEE) style is widely used in writing research papers, commonly in technical fields, particularly in computer science. As for books, it follows this format:

References:

J. K. Author, "Title of Chapter in the Book," in *Title of His Published Book*, xth ed. City of Publisher, Country if not the U.S.A.: Abbrev. of Publisher, Year, pp. xxx–xxx.

For example:

- [1] B. Klaus and P. Horn, *Robot Vision*. Cambridge, MA: MIT Press, 1986.

- [2] L. Stein, "Random Patterns," in *Computers and You*, New York: Wiley, 1994, pp. 55–70.

As for journals, it follows this format:

References:

J. K. Author, "Name of Paper," Abbrev. of *Title of Periodical*, vol. x, no. x, pp. xxx–xxx, Abbrev. of Month, Year.

For example:

- [1] R. E. Kalman, "New Results in Linear Filtering and Prediction Theory," *J. Basic Eng.*, vol. 83, pp. 95–108, Mar., 1961.

- [2] Ye. V. Lavrova, "Geographic Distribution of Ionospheric Disturbance in the F2 Layer," *Tr. Izmiran*, no. 29, pp. 31– 43, Nov. 19, 1961.

Modern Language Association (MLA) style is an academic style guide widely used in the United States, Canada, and other countries, providing guidelines for writing and documentation of research in humanities subjects, such as languages, literary studies, and media studies. As for book with one author, it follows this format:

References:

Author's last name, first name. *Title of Book*. Place of publication: Publisher, Year of publication. Publication medium.

For example:

- McDonagh, Sean. *Why Are We Deaf to the Cry of the Earth*. Dublin: Veritas, 2001. Print.

As for print journal article, it follows this format:

References:

The first author's last name, first name and last author's first name and last name. "Title of Article." *Title of Journal*. Volume. Issue (Year): Pages. Publication medium.

For example:

- Mann, Susan. "Myths of Asian Womanhood." *Journal of Asian Studies.* 59.1 (2000): 835–862. Print.

> **Task**

Decide whether the following statements are true or false based on the passage above.

1) You needn't list all your references at the end of the reference list. (　　)

2) The materials you have paraphrased can't be regarded as the references. (　　)

3) A reference can be used to avoid plagiarism. (　　)

4) A reference list can help readers to locate the materials that have been referred to. (　　)

5) A good reference must be authoritative but not up-to-date. (　　)

6) IEEE style is widely used in computer science while MLA style is especially used in humanities subjects, such as languages, literary studies, and media studies. (　　)

本章配套资源

UNIT 8

Acknowledgements & Submission

Learning Objectives

- To understand the components of an acknowledgement;

- To learn to write an acknowledgement;

- To learn to write a submission cover letter.

Warm-up

Before submitting your paper, please think about the following questions:

- Do you need to write an acknowledgement in your paper? Why or why not?

- How would your paper be processed after submission?

- What should you write in the cover letter when submitting the paper?

Sample Reading

Sample 1

Acknowledgements

Worm strains were provided by the Caenorhabditis Genetics Center. F. C. acknowledges funding from the Wellcome Trust/Royal Society (102531/Z/13/Z and 102531/Z/13/A), C.K. from the German Research Foundation (CRC 1182 "Metaorganisms", Excellence Cluster "Inflammation at Interfaces [EXC306]), H. M. C. from the MRC (MC-A654-5QB90), W. D. H. and L. T. from FWO Flanders, and I. B. from ERC StG 311331 and ERC PoC 842174.* We thank Clara Essmann, Johannes Zimmermann, Ruwen Bohm, and Guido Laucke for technical advice; Kit-Yi Leung and Nicholas Greene for sharing unpublished data; Athanasios Typas, Jürg Bahler, and Irene Miguel-Aliaga for critical reading of the manuscript, and Andrew Osborne for editing the manuscript.

(Pryor, R., et al. 2019. Host-Microbe-Drug-Nutrient Screen Identifies Bacterial Effectors of Metformin Therapy. *Cell*, 178(6): 1299–1312.)

---

* F. C., C. K., H. M. C., W. D. H., L. T., and I. B. are all names of co-authors.

Sample 2

Submission Cover Letter*

Dear Dr. James Joyce,

I am writing to submit our manuscript entitled "A Novel Root-End Filling Material Based on Hydroxyapatite, Tetracalcium Phosphate, and Polyacrylic Acid" by Ling Huchong and Qiao Feng from State Key Laboratory of Bioelectronics, School of Biological Science and Medical Engineering, Southeast University, Nanjing, China. It is submitted to be considered for publication as an "Original Article" in your journal. We developed a novel filling material hydroxyapatite/tetracalcium phosphate/polyacrylic acid cement (HA/TTCP/PAA), which outperformed glass ionomer cement (GIC) and Portland cement (PC) in tests of chemical composition, physical properties, and cytotoxicity.

Given that there are still controversies in the clinical application value of A, B and C, the most common radiopaque agents, we believe that the findings presented in the paper will appeal to dentists and end-filling material developers who subscribe to *International Science Journal*. Although prior studies have identified a few radiopaque agents with which end-filling materials were made and could be used in clinic, they have been cost-prohibitive and difficult to administer on a national level. Thus, our findings will allow your readers to understand chemical composition, physical properties, and cytotoxicity of end-filling materials made from the three agents. In doing so, we hope that our research provides more options for dentists in clinical practice.

No conflict of interest exists in the submission of this manuscript, and the manuscript is approved by all authors for publication. I would like to declare on behalf of my co-authors that the work described was original research that has not been published previously, and not under consideration for publication elsewhere, in whole or in part.

Should you select our manuscript for peer review, we would like to suggest the following potential reviewers/referees because they would have the requisite background to evaluate our findings and interpretations objectively.

1) Duan Yu, University of Texas, Duanyu@utex.edu, Professor of endodontology

2) Shi Tai, University of Texas, Shitai@utex.edu, Professor of endodontology

---

* See Appendix 3 on Page 157 for the paper processing cycle at the editor's office.

Additionally, to the best of our knowledge, neither of the above-suggested persons has any conflict of interest, financial or otherwise.

If you require any additional information regarding our manuscript or any queries, please don't hesitate to contact me at the address below. Thank you for your time and consideration.

Yours sincerely,

Dr. Ling Huchong

Corresponding author:

Prof. Dr. Qiao Feng

State Key Laboratory of Bioelectronics

School of Biological Science and Medical Engineering

Southeast University

Nanjing 210096

P.R. China

Tel: (+8625) 12345678

Fax: (+8625) 12345678

E-mail: Qiao Feng@ seu.edu.cn

> **Tasks**

❶ **List the information elements that you should include in the acknowledgment of a journal paper based on Sample Reading 1.**

_____

_____

_____

_____

❷ List the information elements of a submission cover letter based on Sample Reading 2.

_____

_____

_____

_____

_____

❸ Fill in the blanks according to the Chinese information in the brackets.

The authors 1)_____(感谢) the patients who 2)_____(参与) in the study. We would also like to show our 3)_____(感激) to Dr. Jean-Frederic Colombel (co-director of the Feinstein IBD Center, Mount Sinai Hospital, New York, NY) for invaluable discussions and insights on Crohn's disease, and we thank three 4)_____(匿名评审员) for their detailed 5)_____(修回意见). We are also immensely 6)_____(感激) to Dr. Emilie Grasset (Precision Immunology Institute, Icahn School of Medicine at Mount Sinai, New York, NY) for her 7)_____(专长) and discussion on an earlier version of the 8)_____(稿子). This research 9)_____(部分由……资助) by R01 DK106593, and the Sanford J. Grossman Charitable Trust; R.U. is 10)_____(资助) by a Career Development Award from the Crohn's and Colitis Foundation and an NIH K23 Career Development Award (K23KD111995-01A1).

III Language Focus

Politeness

Politeness in letter/e-mail writing involves taking into account the correspondent's feelings. Therefore, it is always necessary to avoid any choice of words that might be face-threatening when you write a submission cover letter or respond to a reviewer's comments. The table below shows the frequently used speech acts and politeness strategies in correspondence with the editor's office.

Acts	Politeness Strategies	Examples
Salutation	Use appropriate forms of address	Dear Dr. James Joyce
Closing	Use appropriate forms of address	Kind regards
Signature	Use appropriate forms of address	Prof. Dr. Qiao Feng
Context	Establish common ground	As we all know, ... As you would agree, ... As the reviewer suggests that...
	Announce	Thank you for the message... Special thanks to you for your invaluable comments.
Pre-closing	Be optimistic	Look forward to hearing from you.
Enclose	Sender asserts knowledge	Attached is the following... Please find attached the manuscript.
Confirmation	Minimize imposition	I agree with you regarding...
	Establish common ground	It's really true as the reviewer suggests that... We have made correction according to the reviewers' comments. Considering the reviewers' comments, we have...
Request	Announce	I would appreciate it if you could...
	Minimize imposition	Please let me know if...

(Continued)

Acts	Politeness Strategies	Examples
	Hedged	Can you please... I wonder if you could...
Apology	Beg forgiveness	I am sorry for negligence of.../for my incorrect writing...

(Adapted from Goudarzi E., Ghonsooly B., Taghipour Z. 2015. Politeness Strategies in English Business Letters: A Comparative Study of Native and Non-Native Speakers of English. *Psychology of Language and Communication*, 19(1): 44–57.)

> Tasks

❶ **The following sentences are taken from reviewers' comments. Make a point-by-point response to the comments with reference to the expressions listed in the table above.**

1) The entire manuscript needs to be edited for proper use of the English language and syntax.

2) Check instructions for authors for the required journal format for referring to the published literature.

3) Avoid the use of +/– to express variation.

4) The sample size of included studies may be shown in the forest plots (Figure 2).

5) Methods: The reference standard investigations ("gold standard" investigation for final diagnosis) used in the studies may be briefly described.

_____

_____

❷ Fill in the blanks by translating the Chinese information in the brackets.

1) _____. (感谢您指出这一点)

2) _____(请告知) if you have any questions.

3) _____. (稿件请见附件)

4) _____ (我将感激不尽) if you could reply soon.

5) We have made corrections_____. (根据评审的意见)

Ⅳ Academic Writing Skills

A. Writing a Submission Cover Letter

The submission cover letter gives the first impression of your paper and it may help the editor-in-chief to make a decision about whether your paper can be published.

It is a good opportunity for the author to highlight the merits and significance of his or her research. Also it gives the editor a reason to read it further and send it to the peer reviewers. If your research cannot interest the editor, it cannot interest the readers either. So a strong and convincing submission cover letter is very important in the paper processing cycle.

> **Task**

Write a submission cover letter for your own manuscript. You can refer to Sample Reading 2.

B. Writing a Reply to the Decision Letter

In the reply to the decision letter, make sure you mention that you have made a point-by-point revision according to the editor-in-chief's and peer reviewers' comments.

The following is the editor-in-chief's decision letter. Fill in the blanks based on the decision letter and then write a reply to it.

From: iejeditor@cardiff.ac.uk

To: Qiao Feng@seu.edu.cn

CC: Ling Huchong@seu.edu.cn

Subject: Manuscript ID IEJ-12-00123, *International Endodontic Journal*

Body:

Dear Dr. Qiao,

Manuscript ID: IEJ-12-00123

Manuscript Title: A Novel Root-End Filling Material Based on Hydroxyapatite, Tetracalcium Phosphate, and Polyacrylic Acid

I have received the comments of the referee(s) and decided that your manuscript requires major changes and then go through the refereeing process again. However, please note that resubmitting your manuscript does not guarantee eventual acceptance.

Should you wish to revise and resubmit your manuscript, please revise your paper taking into account any points they have raised—their comments can be found at the end of this e-mail. Also double check that in the body of the text and in the reference section the names of authors are spelt correctly including any non-English characters where appropriate.

You will be unable to make your revisions online using the originally submitted version of the manuscript. Instead, revise your manuscript on your PC/MAC using your word processing programme and save it on your computer. Please highlight the changes to your manuscript within the document by using the "track changes" mode in MS Word or the equivalent.

To upload your revised manuscript, log on to http://mc.manuscriptcentral.com/iej and enter your Author Center, where you will find your original manuscript title listed under "Manuscripts with Decisions". Under "Actions", click on "Create a Revision". Your manuscript number has been appended to denote a revision.

When submitting your revised manuscript, you will be able to respond to the comments made by the referees(s) in the space provided. You can use this space to document any changes that you have made to the original manuscript. Please be as specific as possible in your response to the referee(s).

I look forward to receiving your revised manuscript.

Kind regards

Paul Dummer

Editor-in-Chief, *International Endodontic Journal*

iejeditor@cardiff.ac.uk

1) Editor-in-chief's decision: _____

2) The author should:

_____

_____

_____

_____

3) A reply to the decision letter:

Dear

本章配套资源

Appendix 1

A Sample Proposal

Under What Conditions Does Explicit Knowledge of a Second Language Facilitate the Acquisition of Implicit Knowledge? A Research Proposal

Jan H. Hulstijn & Rick de Graaff

Vrije Universiteit Amsterdam

Abstract: This paper proposes nine hypotheses for empirical research aiming to assess under which conditions explicit grammar instruction helps the acquisition of implicit knowledge of a second language. The results of empirical studies, designed on the basis of these hypotheses, may replace the unqualified interface and noninterface positions by qualified positions claiming that explicit instruction facilitates the acquisition of implicit knowledge under specific conditions. These conditions depend on factors such as linguistic domain, complexity, scope and reliability, and semantic or formal redundancy of the target structures. Finally, they depend on factors such as rule versus item learning and reception versus production.

1. Introduction

In this paper we take an empirical approach to the question to what extent the acquisition of implicit knowledge, as the product and goal of second language (L2) learning, can be facilitated by explicit learning. We use the term "explicit learning" in the sense defined by Schmidt, as learning with awareness at the point of learning. According to Schmidt, explicit learning may vary from spontaneous rule discovery by the learner on the one hand to explicit instruction on the other hand, i.e., guidance on the part of the teacher through input enhancement or presentation and explanation of grammar rules.

Some researchers take the stance that explicit grammar instruction is of little help and that L2 acquisition must be fostered by giving L2 learners large amounts of "comprehensible input" (e.g., Krashen, 1981, 1982, 1985). Others recognize the prime importance of large amounts of comprehensible input and involvement of L2 learners in communicative activities, but take the view that, under certain conditions, explicit grammar instruction, in one way or another, can be of considerable help (e.g., Bley-Vroman, 1988; Doughty, 1991; Ellis, 1990, 1993a, 1993b; Larsen-Freeman, 1991; Larsen-Freeman & Long, 1991; Lightbown & Spada, 1993; Schmidt, 1988, 1990, 1993; Rutherford & Sharwood Smith, 1985; Sharwood Smith, 1993; Terrell, 1991; Van Patten & Cadiemo, 1993a, 1993b).

Our perspective is a programmatic one: Assuming that the answer to the question of whether explicit grammar instruction facilitates the acquisition of implicit knowledge will not be an unqualified "never" nor an unqualified "always", how can we lay out a programme of research which aims at assessing when, i.e., under which conditions, explicit grammar instruction helps?

This paper is set up as follows. Section 2 lists our assumptions and summarizes and discusses various theoretical positions: Krashen's (1981, 1982, 1985) noninterface position, Anderson's (1980, 1982) strong interface position, and Ellis' (1993a) weak interface hypothesis. Section 3 provides a number of testable hypotheses, based on various theoretical and pedagogical considerations. Section 4 discusses the relative merits of "natural" versus (semi)artificial experiments. In section 5, we draw our conclusions.

2. Theoretical Positions

Let us summarize the assumptions underlying most current theories of L1 and L2 acquisition. We sum these assumptions up, couched in our own terminology:

(1) Fluent language proficiency of native speakers of any age is based on "implicit knowledge" (I-knowledge) of the grammar of their L1.

(2) Most native speakers have little "explicit knowledge" (E-knowledge) of their L1, although some E-knowledge may be learned in school.

(3) Almost nothing is known about the process of the acquisition of I-knowledge of the L1. One thing is certain, however, caretakers do not teach young children grammar rules. Thus, I-knowledge is not acquired through the acquisition of E-knowledge.

(4) As in the case of L1, a fluent use of the L2 is based on I-knowledge of that language. The behavioral correlate of this I-knowledge is fluency in language use.

The next subsections consider these positions in more detail.

2.1 The Noninterface Position

One of the best known proponents of the noninterface position is Krashen (1981, 1982, 1985). According to Krashen, there is a fundamental difference between "acquisition" (of I-knowledge) and "learning" (of E-knowledge). Learning does not facilitate acquisition. L2-utterances are generated on the basis of I-knowledge. E-knowledge only plays a role in monitoring utterances thus generated. Grammar instruction may result in E-knowledge but cannot result in, nor affect I-knowledge. For that reason, grammar instruction is of little or no importance for becoming fluent in the L2. I-knowledge can only be acquired by receiving large amounts of "comprehensible input". That is about all the noninterface position has to say about the mechanics of the actual process of acquiring I-knowledge. In this respect, Krashen's position reflects Chomsky's much quoted statement (1970), viz. "that we should probably try to create a rich linguistic environment for the intuitive heuristics that the normal human automatically possesses".

Krashen's noninterface position certainly is a well defendable position for L2 pedagogy. But from an empirical perspective it is a fruitless position, as long as the distinction between acquisition and learning has not been operationalized (Hulstijn, 1984; Larsen-Freeman & Long, 1991; McLaughlin 1978, 1987).

2.2 The Interface Position

The interface position comes in two forms (Larsen-Freeman & Long, 1991). First, E-knowledge becomes I-knowledge through practice. Second, E-knowledge cannot become I-knowledge but it aids the acquisition of I-knowledge. Thus, the interface position sees E-knowledge as either necessary or instrumental in acquiring I-knowledge. We will discuss each form in turn.

2.2.1 A Strong Interface Position

According to what Ellis (1993a) has called the "strong interface position", I-knowledge emerges from E-knowledge directly, i.e., through practice. This position is derived from the literature on skill acquisition in cognitive psychology, in particular theories of controlled and automatic processing. One of the best known of these theories is Anderson's ACT theory (Anderson, 1982). According to Anderson, declarative, propositional knowledge is converted into procedural knowledge by processes of compilation, tuning, and restructuring. The original declarative knowledge need not always be replaced by procedural knowledge: "Sometimes the two forms of knowledge can coexist side by side, as when we can speak a foreign language fluently and still remember many rules of grammar. However, it is the procedural, not the declarative knowledge that governs the skilled performance" (Anderson, 1980).

For many years, the strong interface position was the accepted view of most practitioners in the field of L2 pedagogy. A skilled and fluent command of the L2 was (and, by many, still is) viewed as the automatization of the application of explicit grammar rules. It should be noticed, however, that most educationalists interpreted the notion of automatization as rapid serial execution rather than as parallel processing.

2.2.2 A Weak Interface Position

Ellis (1993a) rejects the strong interface position while replacing it by what he calls a "weak interface position". To illustrate all three positions (noninterface, strong interface, and weak interface), Ellis presents the following figure, using labels from both Anderson's skill acquisition theory (1982) and Bialystok's two-dimensional model of language proficiency (see e.g., Bialystok, 1990a, 1991).

Table 1　The Difference Between Explicit/Implicit and Declarative/Procedural Knowledge

	Declarative	**Procedural**
Explicit	*Type A* Conscious knowledge of L2 items.	*Type B* Conscious knowledge of learning, production, and communication strategies. The learner can use explicit knowledge easily and rapidly.
Implicit	*Type C* Intuitive knowledge of L2 items.	*Type D* Ability to employ learning, production, and communication strategies automatically. The learner can use intuitive knowledge fluently.

Source: Ellis, 1993a, p. 94.

3. The Interface Position Translated into Testable Hypotheses

Basing empirical research on the assumption that explicit instruction (and hence that explicit learning) somehow "facilitates" the acquisition of I-knowledge does not mean that we have no theories or other sources of knowledge to draw upon. In this section, we present six dimensions within which variables can be chosen for the formulation of testable research questions. An illustrative example is given for each dimension, followed by one or more testable hypotheses.

From the outset, however, it must be emphasized that each hypothesis embodies a simplification: The reader has to add the phrase "ceteris paribus" to each hypothesis, as it were. In reality, however, all other things aren't equal. A factor mentioned in one hypothesis may well interact with a factor mentioned in another hypothesis. Indeed, it is likely that cases of interaction constitute more interesting issues to be pursued than the straight ones covered by the hypotheses below.

3.1 Linguistic Domain

The first dimension within which one must specify the interface position is linguistic. In which linguistic domains can explicit instruction help the acquisition of I-knowledge? In the domain of morpho-phonology? In the subdomain of lexical, flectional morphology only (e.g., verb conjugation, noun declension)? In syntax? In certain limited areas within syntax only (e.g., word order phenomena related to L1/L2 differences at the level of D-structure, in contrast to S-structure)?

Given the current state of linguistics, one of the most important criteria to distinguish, in a principled way, between various linguistic domains, is offered by Generative Grammar. Generative grammarians distinguish between formal aspects of grammar within the domain of Universal Grammar and domains falling outside the UG scope. Concerning the UG aspects of grammar, our hypotheses might depend on our stance on the issue of whether UG is still available to L2 learners or not. In the former case, parameter resetting is possible. In the latter case, L2 learners will depend more on general cognitive capacities to overcome the loss of the ability to acquire the L2 grammar on the basis of positive L2 input alone. If we assume that UG is still available, our hypotheses might depend on whether the L1 setting of a parameter constitutes a subset or a superset of the L2 setting. In the latter case, L2 learners have to "unlearn" the marked L1 setting, and this may require receiving negative evidence. If a parameter has two possible settings only (e.g., the Head-position parameter, which can either be head-initial or head-final), one is found in L1 and the other in L2, the acquisition of the L2 setting may be possible on the basis of primary linguistic input (positive evidence) only. Finally, when various rules cluster under a single parameter, teaching all rules may not be necessary and even fruitless after one rule has been acquired (Rutherford, 1989; White, 1992;

Schwartz, 1993; Jordens, 1993).

Here are some tentative hypotheses which could be tested on the basis of the above considerations:

* H1: The advantage of the provision of explicit instruction, in comparison with the nonprovision of explicit instruction, is greater in the case of aspects falling outside the scope of UG than in the case of aspects falling inside its scope.

* H2: The advantage of explicit instruction is greater when the L1 setting of a parameter forms a superset and the L2 setting a subset of a parameter than in the reverse situation. With "is greater" in these two and all following hypotheses we mean that the acquisition of I-knowledge with the help of explicit instruction takes place more easily and in less time than without. We do not claim, however, that explicit instruction (and learning) will always result in a higher level of ultimate attainment. Note that, for ease of reading, we have left out the phrase "in comparison with the non-provision of explicit instruction" in hypothesis 2 and all following hypotheses.

3.2 Complexity

The basic idea here is that L2 grammar rules, represented in a declarative, propositional form (as they appear in course books, for example), differ in complexity. Complexity here is not to be defined in terms of linguistic theory, but in cognitive terms.

Consider the following two fabricated examples, illustrating complexity differences between two purely formal (phonological) rules and two semantic (aspectual) rules respectively. Example 1: In language M, verbs have different endings for two aspects, perfect and nonperfect; in language N, however, verbs have different inflections for three aspects, perfective, durative, and punctual. Example 2: In language X there are two plural suffixes for nouns: the suffix -s is added to singular nouns ending on a vowel, and the suffix -os is added to nouns ending on a consonant. Language Y has the same two suffixes: -s for nouns ending on a vowel and for nouns ending on a consonant containing a front vowel in the penultimate syllable, -os for nouns ending on a consonant and containing a back vowel in the penultimate syllable. If we were to make flowcharts for the derivation of inflections in languages M and N and for the derivation of the plural suffix in languages X and Y, the charts for languages M and X would contain fewer steps than those for N and Y respectively. Note that degree of complexity is contingent not so much on the number of forms in a paradigm, but rather on the number (and/or the type) of criteria to be applied in order to arrive at the correct form. On such a declarative notion of complexity, we may base the following hypothesis:

* H3: The advantage of explicit instruction is greater in the case of complex rules than in the case of simple rules.

The reason is that simple formal phenomena may be salient enough in the input to be discovered by L2 learners spontaneously, without the help of explicit instruction. In the case of complex phenomena, however, explicit instruction may save learners considerable time in discovering their intricacies. Note that this hypothesis is concerned with the (cognitive) complexity of a rule of language, not with the complexity of the way in which the rule is explained by teacher or textbook. Of course, it is a sound pedagogical principle that explanations should be formulated in as simple as possible terms. Furthermore, declarative complexity as defined here, is not to be confused with "complicatedness" or "difficulty", experienced by learners as a result of contrast between their L1 and L2 (see also H2).

Some researchers have tried to explain the notion of cognitive complexity in terms of processing constraints (Clahsen, 1984; Pienemann, 1989; Pienemann & Johnston, 1987). This was done to explain so called "natural" acquisition orders, found among L2 learners who did not receive formal L2 instruction. The hypotheses of Pienemann are of an entirely different nature than the one proposed here. The former hypotheses are embedded in a developmental theory pertaining to acquisition orders. Our claim that explicit instruction helps more in the case of complex rules than in the case of simple rules pertains to the ease and duration of acquisition, not to the rank order of acquisition onset times of structural features.

3.3 Scope and Reliability

Many rules of language apply only probabilistically. Such "rules", or "probabilistic tendencies" can differ in scope (the number of cases covered) and reliability (the extent to which the rule holds true, Bates & MacWhinney, 1989). Scope may be large or small and reliability may be high or low. Let us draw two (arbitrary) border lines: The scope of a rule is said to be large or small when the rule covers more or fewer than 50 cases; the rehability of a rule is said to be high or low when the rule applies in more or less than 90% of all cases. According to these definitions, there are four possibilities. Consider the following examples concerning noun gender in German (*mascuhne, feminine*, and *neuter*), as specified by Mills (1986: 33):

(1) Of the ca. 15,000 singular nouns ending on -*e*, about 13,500 (90%) are feminine.

(2) Of the 15 monosyllabic nouns beginning with *Kn*-, 14 are masculine (93%).

(3) Of the 107 monosyllabic nouns ending on $-C_{nasal} C$, 75 are masculine (70%).

(4) Of the 45 nouns ending on *-ier*, 27 are neuter (60%).

We can classify these four tendencies in terms of scope and reliability, as follows:

(1) = large scope & high reliability

(2) = small scope & high reliability

(3) = large scope & low reliability

(4) = small scope & low reliability

Many language teachers believe that it makes sound practice to restrict explicit grammar teaching to rules with both a large scope and a high reliability. In the three remaining cases, learners should not be given the rules. Such rules are believed to bring too little profit considering their costs (the law of "diminishing return"). Thus, in the cases of (2), (3), and (4), learners must be told to simply associate the gender feature to each word individually. On this practice we may base the following hypothesis:

*H4: The advantage of explicit instruction is greater when a rule applies to many cases (large scope) and when it has a high success rate (high reliability) than when it has a small scope and/or a low reliability.

Note that complexity on the one hand and scope and reliability on the other, although to be distinguished conceptually, in the practice of language pedagogy often go hand in hand. For instance, language teachers often decide not to present complex rules if they are small in scope. Furthermore, when teachers wonder whether they should explain a phenomenon either with a more reliable but more complex rule or with a less reliable but more simple rule, they may opt for the latter, sacrificing reliability for simplicity, e.g., presenting a general rule without its exceptions or subrules.

3.4 Rule Learning Versus Item Learning

Consider the following four rules of German:

1. The finite verb in declarative main sentences almost always takes second position.

2. When only one constituent is being negated, the negation word *nicht* is placed immediately before it, e.g., *nicht A sondern B* ("not A but B").

3. German nouns ending on *-e* are almost always feminine, as we have already seen; e.g., *Küche* ("kitchen") is feminine.

4. Verb forms in the present tense, indicative, first person singular almost always end on *-e*; e.g., *ich lerne Englisch* ("I learn English").

All four rules are large in scope and they rank high on reliability. Yet there is a difference between rules 1 and 2 on the one hand and rules 3 and 4 on the other. For the latter two phenomena, there are, in principle, two ways for language production. The language user may either apply the rule, or produce individually stored forms (e.g., *lerne*) or features (e.g., the feature Feminine with *Küche*). Thus, for phenomena 3 and 4, two alternative routes towards language production offer themselves, one based on rule learning and one based on item learning. For phenomena 1 and 2, however, there is only the possibility of rule application. One could argue that teaching rules 3 and 4 does not foster language acquisition much, since learners may spontaneously learn individual forms or individual features (item learning). For phenomena 1 and 2, however, rule teaching may help learners to apply the principle (which may or may not have originated from previous encounters with a number of individual instances) to an indefinitely large class of instances. This leads to the following hypothesis:

*H5: The advantage of explicit instruction is greater when language production can only be based on rule application, than when it can be based not only on rule application but also on the retrieval of individually stored items ("item learning"). The likelihood of item learning as an alternative to rule learning may be dependent of the frequency with which items occur. Forms occurring frequently in the input may be more likely to be stored and accessed separately than infrequent forms. Since the issue of item v.s. rule learning mostly pertains to inflectional morphology, a hypothesis concerning the relative merits of item learning might be more relevant for the learning of languages with moderate flection (French, German, English) than for the learning of languages with high amounts of flection (Turkish, Finnish, Hungarian). Thus, we can reiterate the above stated complexity hypothesis, while applying it to the domain of flection:

*H6: The advantage of explicit instruction is greater in the case of complex inflectional rules (which are also reliable and large in scope) than in the case of simple inflectional rules (also reliable and large in scope).

There are two motivations for this hypothesis. The first reason is that grammar instruction may be more helpful to clarify complex, less salient structures than to clarify simple, more salient structures (section 3.2). The second reason is that, if there are fewer forms in an inflectional paradigm, each one of them is more likely to occur more often and is therefore more likely to be learned individually, than if there are more forms per paradigm. In the latter case, each form is likely to occur less frequently than all forms together, and is therefore less likely to be learned as an individual item.

3.5 Reception Versus Production

There is ample evidence that L2 learners often keep making errors in spontaneous speech long after the grammar rule in question has been presented and practiced in written exercises. In fact, it is on the basis of such evidence that proponents of the noninterface position argue that explicit instruction in L2 pedagogy is of little importance and should perhaps be abandoned altogether. It is surprising, however, that the debate of whether explicit instruction is useful or not, focuses exclusively on E-knowledge's impact on speaking and writing and almost never on its impact on reading and listening. One might argue, however, that E-knowledge (and hence explicit instruction) affects language comprehension during reading and listening positively, in that it helps L2 learners to discern the meaning of the input. Thus, although we might acknowledge that explicit instruction has limited effect on language production, we may hypothesize that explicit instruction has considerable effect on language comprehension.

*H7: The advantage of explicit instruction is greater in the case of L2 comprehension than in the case of L2 production.

3.6 Semantic Versus Formal Redundancy

Some language forms are semantically redundant (e.g., the -s suffix in third person singular verb forms in English) while others are not (e.g., the -s plural noun suffix in English). This may be of more importance to language comprehension than to language production, since knowledge of semantically redundant phenomena may not be required for language comprehension. Hence, we frame the following hypothesis:

*H8: As for L2 comprehension, the advantage of explicit instruction is greater in the case of grammatical features with semantic implications than in the case of purely formal (semantically redundant) features.

In language production on the other hand, learners may have more difficulty to apply purely formal rules (e.g., adding third person singular -s to English present tense verb forms) than to apply combined formal-semantic rules (e.g., adding a plural -s to count nouns in English). Terrell (1991) states that explicit grammar instruction helps to segment the otherwise overwhelming input and to establish meaning-form links, especially for morphology that is neither salient nor semantically essential. This leads us to the following hypothesis:

*H9: As for L2 production, the advantage of explicit instruction is greater in the case of purely formal (semantically redundant) features than in the case of grammatical features with semantic implications.

4. Laboratory Versus Natural Settings: A Twin Approach

In the previous sections we have shown that the empirical study of the influence of grammar instruction on I-knowledge is a complicated affair. One of the most notorious methodological problems is to adequately manipulate all those independent variables which one wants to manipulate while keeping all other potentially interfering variables constant. This is almost impossible in "normal" classrooms with real L2 learners (Harley, this issue). It comes as no surprise, therefore, that the outcomes of such studies often form the object of considerable disagreement. This was recently illustrated by the controversy between Lightbown & Pienemann (1993) and Krashen (1993). Although research in "real" classrooms should bring the final proof because of the alleged validity of the classroom setting, a researcher may want to exert more control than is possible in a normal classroom setting.

There are various ways to bring instruction and learning under control of the researcher. The first way is to control the language to be learned. This can be done by teaching an artificial or partly artificial language (e.g., Issidorides, 1988; Hulstijn, 1989b; Yang & Givon, 1993; DeKeyser, 1994). The advantage of this method is that the researcher can be certain that no subject in the experiment can have knowledge of the target structures and that performance on tests must stem from learning during the experiment.

The second way is to control the instruction properly (i.e., the explanation of grammar rules). One way of doing this is to replace the live explanation of the teacher by a prerecorded explanation. Using a computer-controlled learning setting is an obvious way of controlling instruction (Doughty, 1991).

Finally, the researcher may control input in a quantitative way by specifying in advance how much instruction and practice subjects will receive. Here again, a computer-controlled learning setting presents itself as an obvious choice (e.g., Chapelle & Jamieson, 1986; Yang & Givon, 1993).

Does this mean that hypotheses such as the ones advanced in section 3 should only be investigated in "unnatural", laboratory settings? Certainly not. The final proof should always be given in a "normal" language class, with "real" teachers and "real" L2 learners, learning a "real" L2 in the framework of a "real" language course, including "normal" exchanges between teacher and learners and among learners themselves (see Van Lier, this issue). However, for methodological reasons it may be recommendable to also conduct more laboratory-type of experiments in which the researcher can exert control of the targets to be learned, the instruction and the execution of receptive and productive tasks, both quantitatively and qualitatively. Natural learning experiments may score high on validity but are likely to score low on reliability. (Semi)artificial learning experiments may score high on reliability but are likely to score low on validity. That is why, in our own research, we adopt a so called twin approach, combining an artificial or semi-artificial experiment with a "natural" experiment (Hulstijn, 1989a, 1989b, 1992, 1993).

5. Conclusions

One of the most nagging questions which has haunted researchers and practitioners alike for a long time, is the question of whether grammar instruction aids L2 acquisition or not. The aim of this contribution was to show that it is highly unlikely that this question can ever be answered with an unqualified "yes" or "no". With the aid of the distinctions proposed by Schmidt between explicit knowledge, explicit learning and explicit instruction, and working in the framework of an interface position between explicit and implicit knowledge, we have tried to demonstrate that it is possible to formulate a fair number of hypotheses, specifying under what conditions explicit knowledge may facilitate the acquisition of implicit knowledge. Our second aim was to demonstrate that it is possible to go beyond the stage of claiming (on the basis of acquisition theories or pedagogical experiences and intuitions) that explicit knowledge may or may not help acquisition. Many hypotheses can and should be tested empirically. The preceding sections lay out a vast research program. It is our hunch that the results of empirical studies, conducted in laboratories as well as in "real" classrooms, will replace the unqualified interface and noninterface positions, which have hitherto dominated the debate, by qualified positions. These conditions depend on factors such as linguistic domain, complexity, scope and reliability, and semantic or formal redundancy of the target structures. And finally, they depend on factors such as rule versus item learning, reception versus production.

References: *omitted*

A Suggested Schedule for a Short-Term Research

It is impossible to produce a schedule that exactly matches every student's research paper assignment. But generally there are 11 distinct steps in the process, requiring you to submit at least 8 hand-ins over a period of 15 weeks. With some variations, many instructors observe the following schedule:

What You Must Do	What You Must Produce	When It Is Due
1) You must select a topic that is complex enough to be researched from a variety of sources but narrow enough to be covered in 10 or so pages.	Two acceptable topics, one of which the instructor will approve	At the end of the 2nd week
2) You must do the exploratory scanning and reading of sources on your topic, and propose several research questions that could be answered within the required length of the paper.	2–3 research questions	At the end of the 4th week
3) You must gather information on your topic and assemble it into some usable sequence.	A literature review, a thesis statement, and an outline	At the end of the 8th week
4) You must draft a literature review, a thesis statement expressing the major idea behind your paper.	A literature review, a thesis statement, and an outline	At the end of the 8th week
5) You must outline the major parts of your paper.	A literature review, a thesis statement, and an outline	At the end of the 8th week

(Continued)

What You Must Do	What You Must Produce	When It Is Due
6) You must collect data if it is an empirical study or report.	Methodology	At the end of the 9th week
7) You must analyze the data.	Results	At the end of the 10th week
8) You must discuss the findings and draw a conclusion.	Discussion and conclusion	At the end of the 11th week
9) You must write a rough draft of the paper arguing, proving, or supporting your hypothesis with information uncovered by your research. You must acknowledge all borrowed ideas, data, and opinions.	A rough draft of the paper	At the end of the 13th week
10) You must prepare a bibliography or reference listing all sources used in the paper.	The paper, complete with bibliography or references	At the end of the 14th week
11) You must revise and edit the draft according to the requirements.	The revised paper	At the end of the 15th week

Paper Processing Cycle

The flowchart below explains the manuscript processing cycle. Once the manuscript is submitted for publication, it is subjected to screening, quality assessment, reviewing, and further production processing involving language assessment, figure improvement, preparation of proofs and incorporation of required corrections.

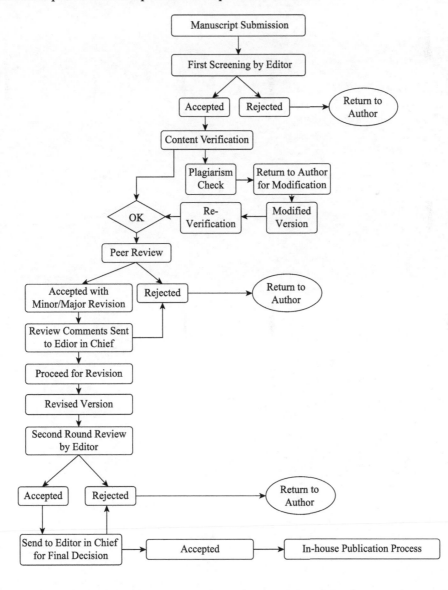